Making Choices in Christ

Making Choices in Christ
The Foundations of Ignatian Spirituality

Joseph A. Tetlow, SJ

LOYOLA PRESS.
A JESUIT MINISTRY
CHICAGO

LOYOLA PRESS.
A JESUIT MINISTRY
3441 N. ASHLAND AVENUE
CHICAGO, ILLINOIS 60657
(800) 621-1008
WWW.LOYOLAPRESS.ORG

Scripture quotations are taken from the Jerusalem Bible © by Darton, Longman & Todd, Ltd., and Doubleday & Company, Inc., 1966, 1967, and 1968. Reprinted with permission.

Cover photo © Sindre Ellingsen/Getty
Cover design by Kathryn Seckman Kirsch
Interior design by Maggie Hong

Library of Congress Cataloging-in-Publication Data
Tetlow, Joseph A.
  Making choices in Christ : the foundations of Ignatian spirituality / Joseph A. Tetlow.
    p. cm.
  Includes bibliographical references.
  ISBN-13: 978-0-8294-2716-5
  ISBN-10: 0-8294-2716-3
  1. Ignatius, of Loyola, Saint, 1491-1556. Exercitia spiritualia.
  2. Spirituality—Catholic Church. 3. Spiritual exercises. 4. Spiritual life—Catholic Church. I. Title.
  BX2179.L8T445 2008
  248.3—dc22

                                                              2008000639

Printed in the United States of America
08 09 10 11 12 13 Versa 10 9 8 7 6 5 4 3 2 1

For colleagues
Jesuit and lay
who invite me to work with them
and let me work for them
who in the Holy Spirit have become
friends in the Lord

Contents

Introduction

It was my great privilege to work as assistant to Fr. Peter-Hans Kolvenbach, SJ, superior general of the Society of Jesus, for Ignatian spirituality. My base for more than eight years was Rome, but the position took me to scores of retreat houses and spirituality centers on every continent. It gave me access to Jesuits and laypeople who live and spread Ignatian spirituality. My commission meant listening to their experiences so as to spread abroad how the Spiritual Exercises are being practiced and how Ignatian spirituality is developing.

My background in American philosophy was a great advantage, since it attends carefully to experience and its processes. At the same time, I stand in the long line of those who have been guided through the Exercises—a line that reaches all the way back to Master Ignatius. The experience of the Exercises, now as then, shapes a way of living in Christ Jesus that we now call Ignatian spirituality.

This book attempts a sketch of that spirituality as it is being lived around the world today. It will help those who wonder what really lies behind this "Jesuit mystique." It will inform those who have made the Spiritual Exercises—the prolonged and distinctively structured prayer experience—of how their experiences express the depths of Christ's revelation. It may guide those who are studying the text of *The Spiritual Exercises*—the oldest handbook still applicable in real time.

Ignatian spirituality, as everyone knows, begins in the experience of the Spiritual Exercises of Ignatius of Loyola. For long decades, the "real" Exercises were the preserve of Jesuits and other religious. No more. Today, men and women, religious and lay, young and elderly, Roman Catholics and Christians of other churches are praying through the Exercises and also giving them to others. They are doing this in the three different ways that Master Ignatius described in the opening paragraphs of his little book *Annotations*. It might be useful to note these ways here; skip the next paragraphs if you are already familiar with them.

The first way he describes (Annotation 18) helps Christians interiorize the truths they live by and structure for themselves a truly Christian way of life. Ignatius used this way a great deal during his fifteen years as a layman and continued to do so even long after his ordination as a priest.

The second way (Annotation 19), as it is done now, requires a person to pray daily for some long weeks and months, following the structure of revealed truths that Master Ignatius outlined for the full thirty-day retreat. The retreatant begins by reflecting on creation in Christ Jesus and moves through human sinfulness and the need for redemption. He or she then contemplates Jesus of Nazareth's incarnation, public life, passion, and resurrection. These Exercises, now universally referred to as the Nineteenth Annotation retreat, or the Exercises in daily life, help people reach a serious decision or make deep changes in their way of living. In my experience, the Nineteenth Annotation retreat is the most common way of giving and going through the Exercises in use today.

The third way of making the Spiritual Exercises (Annotation 20) is the "long retreat" of thirty or more days in silence and seclusion. This retreat is now made in a retreat house, often with others. It is directed by trained guides—once only by Jesuits, but now just as often by other religious or by laymen or laywomen. This is the way Master Ignatius took his first companions through the Exercises. They all chose to give their lives to Christ and moved toward forming the Society of Jesus, the Jesuit order. Every Jesuit does this long retreat twice during his formative years. It is notable that many laymen and laywomen are making this retreat as they come to important changes in midlife.

All three of these ways are now practiced everywhere. Consequently, more people give and make St. Ignatius's Spiritual Exercises today than ever before. Laypeople are confirmed in this ministry in a way unparalleled since Master Ignatius, as a layman himself, instructed some to pass on their experiences.

Within all of these activities lies an appreciation of the revelation given in and through Jesus of Nazareth and a distinctive set of prayer forms and practices that make up Ignatian spirituality. Underlying Ignatian spirituality is a rich and complex spiritual theology, extraordinarily available for what we might call ordinary people, which is the subject of this book.

These pages owe a lot to a great number of people who generously shared their experiences and wisdom with me. I can name only these few, who will know why they belong specially in this book: Donald L. Gelpi, SJ, of Berkeley, California; Roswitha Cooper of Munich and Rome; David Coghlan, SJ, of Dublin; Michael Smith, SJ, of Melbourne; Jim and Joan Felling of Vancouver and St. Louis; Mary Mondello of St. Louis; Jenny Go of Manila and San Francisco; Gérôme Gagnier, SJ, of Addis Ababa and Rome; Thomas Rochford, SJ, of Denver and Rome; Annemarie Poulin-Cambell of Johannesburg; Raul Paiva, SJ, of Itaici, Brazil; and, before all the rest, Fr. Peter-Hans Kolvenbach, general of the Society of Jesus.

Seeking an Active God

Spirituality shows up often enough in the public square as a vague postmodern fashion designed to replace worn-out religions. The reality is no such vague and shopworn thing. Rather, as a personal quest for the transcendent holy One, spirituality runs through all the great cultures. Although the word *spirituality* was coined just a few centuries ago, the quest left its record in humankind's most ancient art and architecture, writing and legislating. In the media today, the word can mean quite different things: an indistinct feeling about meaning in life qualifies just as well as the daily routine of a monk. All along, the traditional spiritualities have organized not only a special worldview and a way of praying but also a way of living.

With singular power and explicitness, spirituality in this sense has characterized Christian cultures from the beginning. It still does. Everywhere, the spiritual traditions of the Benedictines, the Franciscans, and the Dominicans thrive, as they have for many centuries. These traditional spiritualities were first practiced in monasteries and cloisters; then, around the time of Europe's discovery of the Americas, spirituality came out into the marketplace. Ignatius of Loyola was vagabonding there as it did.

Ignatian spirituality, of course, is one of the more recent in the church. This spirituality took the great traditions of the interior life in the cloistered world and brought them to bear on everyday life in the home and on the street. There, in the world, Ignatian spirituality matured thoroughly before being applied to an ordered community life (that of the Jesuits). Even then, it was applied to a "communitas ad dispersionem," as the Jesuit constitutions put it—a community set up explicitly to be dispersed into mission. This spirituality was meant to empower a dynamic service of God out in the marketplace. Here is one of the more obvious reasons why Ignatian spirituality remains useful today, when the whole church is evolving a distinctly lay spirituality.

Ignatian spirituality offers to those of us who live busy lives a way to God. It helps us find our own appropriate way in mental prayer and in an active life in the world and the church. It offers a way to discern what God wishes us to do, both with the whole of our lives as we focus down on a personal vocation and in the many concrete decisions we have to make every day. Its approach to discernment seems particularly helpful now, when we face so many options and our world changes so rapidly. This is because the God whom Ignatian spirituality seeks is an acting God, a busy God who continues to be our Creator and Lord.

Other spiritualities seek the God of love, or of beautiful order, or of truth. Ignatian spirituality seeks the God who is always at work in the world and in each heart. The purpose of the spirituality is to help us find how we are to work along with God to bring the reign of Christ to human life and good order to the natural world—to the everyday world as it now is. We find God working first of all in and through the church as the Spirit has formed it into the present, with all its holiness and sinfulness. Well practiced, this spirituality brings us to an informed,

open-eyed love for the church—for the real church in an ecu-
menical age. Not surprisingly, Ignatian spirituality is proving
helpful not only to cradle Catholics, but to convinced Lutherans,
Presbyterians, Methodists, and Baptists as well. Dedicated evan-
gelicals are astonished to find that Ignatius's Spiritual Exercises
give room for their own kinds of prayer.

Following this spirituality, we take both the church and the
world as they really are. We are not trying to create an orderly life
apart from the joys and sorrows of the everyday world, as though
spirituality were a withdrawal from the world. On the contrary,
we know that we are called to say yes to all that God is putting
into the world and then to find how God wants us to cooperate
in this ongoing creation. We know that the world is still coming
to be, and we are coming to be along with our "life world"—that
is, the world from which we come, in which we live, and to which
we are called to bring justice, peace, and love. Now, in this place
of ours and in our time.

Ignatian spirituality is not only a worldly spirituality but
also a radically lay spirituality. It rose from the experiences of a
layman and was developed for the sake of those who were busily
engaged in everyday life. It began in notes that Ignatius kept
about his own experiences as he was picking his difficult, con-
flicted way (he was tempted to suicide) through concrete choices
to his personal vocation. What was he to do with his life as the
church was going through agonizing reformation and his stone-
walled European world was being blown apart by discoveries of
a broad, lush, round world?

All he knew at the beginning was that he had a peremp-
tory call to find Christ in the world and thereby live a holy life.
Gradually, he discovered that certain materials and kinds of
prayer helped him in specific ways to sort through the effects of
sin in his life and discover honestly what God's love demanded
that he do next. He thought of these materials and kinds of

prayer in the same way his contemporaries thought of them, as "spiritual exercises." Helping others with what he found helpful himself, he then learned from their varied experiences, too. He was a great listener; from the first paragraph in his text, he tells what he learned from other peoples' experiences. In this way, he steadily gave shape to the challenging, fruitful spiritual experience that we call the Spiritual Exercises and cobbled together a way to seek and find the acting God, a way we now call a *spirituality*—Ignatian spirituality.

One Way to God

Ignatius gave the Spiritual Exercises to many others—university students, nobles, religious women and men, and even illiterates. Besides being a passionate lover of Jesus Christ, he was a methodical man and a great note-taker. As he studied at the universities in Salamanca and Paris and helped people in Venice and Rome, he gradually put his notes into a systematic form that he titled simply *The Spiritual Exercises*. He finally printed his text, after the pope had declared it orthodox, in 1548. It is a sort of handbook, surely the oldest one that can still be used in its original form. The reason is simple: it has been used without break ever since it was printed.

Master Ignatius had learned a great deal from the treasures of spirituality in the church, from contemporary Benedictines, Dominicans, Carmelites, and Franciscans whom historians can name. For instance, immobilized for months after being gravely wounded in battle, he lay absorbing Ludolph of Saxony's *Life of Christ*. Ludolph began religious life as a Dominican and then became a Carthusian, and his book draws on all the great traditions in the West. When Master Ignatius began an interior life, he went directly to the great Benedictine monastery of Montserrat and learned from its *Ejercitatorio Spiritualis,* which divides spiritual experience into four "weeks," as Ignatius would later do in his handbook. Through his early years, he learned from Franciscan confessors and Dominican preachers.

When Ignatius began to evangelize people in the plazas, he learned a great deal from them. He was always very careful not to impose on others what had helped him, a mistake he considered the greatest that a spiritual guide or friend can make. Yet he was clear that the revelation made in Jesus Christ, passed on in the church's Scriptures and teaching, was the uniquely secure guide to finding God. Ignatius's way to God is proving helpful in our day, marked as it is by both individualism and the need to rediscover the core truths of Christ's revelation.

Since about 1530, people have been making these Spiritual Exercises and then giving them to others. Ignatius gave them to many laypeople and religious and encouraged them all to pass them on. His companions in forming the Society of Jesus continued the ministry, which has been carried on by Jesuits through four and a half centuries. The result is that today thousands of men and women around the world, certainly more than ever before, have had the experience of prayer and spiritual conversation called the "Ignatian retreat."

During the centuries when only Jesuits gave the retreats, they preached the Exercises to groups instead of giving them to individuals one at a time, the way Master Ignatius gave the full Exercises. These preached retreats were the "Exercises of St. Ignatius" that the church knew before the Second Vatican Council. A number of people would come together—typically, religious for eight days, or groups of laity for a weekend—and a priest would preach four or five times each day (and for a long while), strictly following the outline of the materials in the handbook. This style was used even for the retreats of thirty days. (It made memorable the retreat in 1947 during which I chose to be a Jesuit.)

After the Second Vatican Council, those giving the Exercises went back to Ignatius's original way of giving the Exercises, and a great revolution took place. In the 1960s, putting historical research into practice, Jesuits began once again directing and guiding people one-to-one. Religious and then laity followed into this ministry. Just as radically, all began giving the Exercises not only as closed retreats in silence but also as Master Ignatius had clearly suggested as an alternative, in everyday life. Business professionals and parents no longer needed to go off to the wilderness to pray through the Exercises; they prayed at home or in their workplaces and met regularly with a guide. It is important to note that laymen and laywomen are guiding others in these Exercises, which has not happened much since Ignatius himself urged it. All of these practices have begun reshaping authentic Ignatian spirituality.

3

Three Retreats and a Way of Life

M aster Ignatius did not find it easy to decide how to live his life, and he discovered that few of us do. When we have any options at all, we do not easily choose a vocation. Moreover, we are pulled this way and that by what our life world treasures most and by our own less-than-orderly desiring. This was true in Ignatius's day as the church was reforming during the Council of Trent, and it is true today as the church is reforming after the Second Vatican Council.

When you set out to find what God wants, the experience of the Spiritual Exercises helps put some order into your thinking and desiring. A little more detail about the Exercises will be useful, because the brief meditations in this book will more or less follow their structure.

The primary experience, the "long retreat," takes thirty days, in silence and seclusion. You go somewhere to be alone and move into deep silence—no phones or e-mail. You pray four or five hours a day, using a set frame and following the materials in the handbook. You reflect systematically on your prayer experiences, keep good notes, and meet daily with a guide, who explains the materials and helps you interpret your experiences. If you are trying to decide what to do with your life or to undertake some serious reform, your guide will help you understand the motions in your spirit but will be careful not to influence your choice.

Your prayer is divided into four "Weeks," each of which can last from a few days to ten. In the first of these Weeks, you pray over the basic meaning of human existence. You attend to the mercy of God in the face of human sinfulness and to the way God cherishes you even as you sin. You come to feel that God summons you in a special way to contribute to the building of the reign. Then, in the Second Week, you meditate and contemplate the coming of the Son of God into human flesh and how he lived a human life. In the Third and Fourth Weeks, you enter into his passion and resurrection. At the end, you pray quietly to love the way God loves. This long retreat is described in the Twentieth Annotation, one of the brief numbered paragraphs of instruction at the beginning of Master Ignatius's handbook. It is made today by hundreds of priests, religious, and laymen and laywomen every year, on every continent and in many languages.

Master Ignatius also found, as we find today, that many people had a serious choice to make or a real reform to undertake but could not go off for a month by themselves. So he also arranged to guide people through the Exercises as they continued their everyday life. He would guide them to pray an hour or two each day, taking them through the four Weeks to find what God wanted of them. Guides have found this Nineteenth Annotation retreat helpful everywhere and among all kinds of people. It is probably now the most common form of making the Exercises.

Master Ignatius often gave people only parts of the Exercises because they did not want to make the whole retreat or were not really able to. He described his practice in the Eighteenth Annotation. Many guides today do the same, taking groups through what are commonly called the "Exercises in daily life." These guides are participating in what Pope John Paul II called "the new evangelization," bringing Christians back to the blessed knowledge of Jesus Christ. Like Master Ignatius, they are recommending to ordinary Catholics a fundamentally Christian way of life—the Ignatian way of living in the church.

The Ignatian way is simply this: You receive regularly the sacraments of communion and reconciliation. You examine your thoughts, words, and actions every day, making sure that your conscience is well-informed and matured. You pray awhile every day, perhaps in a simple way with the creed, the Our Father, and the commandments. You carefully discern (we'll talk more about this Ignatian process later) your style of life and how your diet respects your health and service. Rejecting negative self-image and perfectionism, you live joyfully with the gifts that God gives you. And you do everything you can to live faithfully and peacefully within the church. Live this way, and you are practicing Ignatian spirituality the way most people are called to practice it.

4

There Is Only Jesus Christ

Ignatian spirituality begins in the revelation that all things come to be in Jesus Christ. "There is only Christ: he is everything and he is in everything" (Colossians 3:11). The Father is the source and always the One to whom we appeal, as Jesus taught. From the Father, all of creation comes through the Son, "for in him were created all things in heaven and on earth: everything visible and everything invisible, Thrones, Dominations, Sovereignties, Powers" (Colossians 1:16). Jesus himself declared that "the Father, who is the source of life, has made the Son the source of life" (John 5:26).

Ignatius of Loyola was led to God through the *Life of Christ* of Ludolph of Saxony, which he read, reread, and took notes from as he lay on his couch with savagely wounded knees. Ludolph begins his richly detailed reflection on Jesus of Nazareth by referring to him as both *principium* and *fundamentum*. Ignatius's "Principle and Foundation" (paragraph 23 of *The Spiritual Exercises*) has been treated in the past by rationalists as philosophy. This is a little like grinding up Michelangelo's *David* to make a marble brick wall. For Ignatius, praising, reverencing, and loving *Dominum nostrum* were simply actions for *Dominum nostrum Jesum Christum*, as he put it in the Latin translation of the Exercises that he submitted to the pope for the church's approbation. There is no other principle and foundation than Jesus Christ.

Anyone can live a good life in the church without pondering all this very much. When we are guided by the Holy Spirit to choose an active interior life, however, we place on ourselves the obligation of learning the consequences of this truth. For to believe a truth means not merely claiming to believe it, but also accepting its real consequences in action in everyday life.

Well and good. And if we believe that creation began and goes on in Christ by the work of the Holy Spirit, how will we know what the consequences are? We find them by contemplating the life of Jesus of Nazareth. He showed once and for all what happens when a human being encounters the transcendent God. We have a record of that unique life in both Scripture and the church's teaching, and we value it as the irreplaceable source for finding what God is hoping in us and in our life world. For in his fully human life, Jesus showed how you think and feel and act when you freely fulfill everything that God hopes in you and through you.

Jesus of Nazareth declared more than once that his work was not his own, but "it is the Father, living in me, who is doing this work" (John 14:10). And again, "I can do nothing by myself . . . my aim is to do not my own will, but the will of him who sent me" (John 5:30). And finally, "The works my Father has given me to carry out . . . testify that the Father has sent me" (John 5:36). Everything he freely chose to do was according to the Father's hopes in him and in his life world. Even what he knew came from the Father: "the words I say to you I do not speak as from myself" (John 14:10).

The early Christians learned to think of Jesus as the Wisdom of God. They applied to Christ what the book of Wisdom says about Wisdom itself: he "is a reflection of the eternal light, untarnished mirror of God's active power, image of his goodness" (7:26). In following Christ, we try as completely as possible to reflect in our lives the one who is "the image of the unseen God and the first-born of all creation" (Colossians 1:15). So we search his life for the way to find God acting in all things here and now.

Reflecting God the Father's power at work in the world is giving glory to God, for God's glory is precisely his infinite wisdom and power made manifest in concrete worldly events. This is the service that we are called to give to God: to make manifest the work that the Father is doing in the created world. Here is the Christian's deepest identity: we are to be reflections, however fitful and fragmentary, of God's work as he evolves all things under Christ the Head. This is why, in the familiar words, the glory of God is a human person fully alive.

We begin an Ignatian spiritual journey by accepting this intimate relationship freely and with an open (if tremulous) heart. This is the praise and service that God hopes for: not talk or feelings or intentions, but doing what God wants done, in the name of Jesus Christ, for all the world to see. What God wants is a kingdom of justice and peace and love. The divine privilege—*privilege* literally means "freedom from a law"; here, the law of sin and death—granted to us who are baptized into Christ, to the members of this Body, is to continue the work of Jesus of Nazareth, day by day on earth.

Creation and Chaos

E very spirituality is a human way to God, who transcends all human means. The special way of each one circumscribes how those who follow it will know God in Christ, "the Way, the Truth and the Life" (John 14:6). Through a telescope, you can see a million stars but not a single molecule; through a microscope, you can see a molecule, but no stars. If the means you use to know God are faith-filled study and research, you will primarily know God who is Truth. If the means you use is long contemplative quiet, you will primarily know God who is Love. The God in Christ sought by Ignatian spirituality is primarily the Way.

The God whom we seek in Ignatian spirituality is "God our Creator and Lord," as Master Ignatius tended to say—God who is our Creator not in the far distant past, beyond the big bang, but who is now creating us, moment by moment. God is always making you and everything around you, visible and invisible. At every moment, God is your Creator. To follow the Ignatian way, you have to get beyond the child's knowledge: Who made me? God made me. *Made*—at some time in the long-forgotten past.

In the Ignatian way to God, you ask for the grace of a more intimate feeling and mature conviction. How is God your

Creator? The response is that God chose for you your race and nation and still chooses the world events that shape you. God chose your parents. God chose the city where you were born, the day, and even the minute. God has been acting all along in your parents, relations, friends, and teachers to shape the person you now are.

Here is the core truth about God as your Creator and Lord: You are who God wants you to be. God loves you as you are—not as you might be or could be. God loves you because you are who you are, for God is making you who you are. When you know this, you have accepted the most intimate relationship with God that a busy life allows, a relationship that fills all things.

The church has formally declared that God creates all things out of "chaos," in its original Greek sense: nothingness. But the church knows that God goes on creating all things visible and invisible. Hence, God creates you with matter that has been coming to maturity for billions of years. Out of the chaos of molecules in your parents' bodies, God assembled your tiny self, and in your mother's womb taught you to take from the chemical chaos you floated in just those molecules that your body needed in order to grow. Out of the chaos of sound, God created words for you to understand and use. From the chaos of loving gestures and frustrated infantile desires, God drew you into reason and rationality. All those realities in your self that you never chose God chose in you and for you.

God the Creator and Lord is creating each one of us in all intimate particulars; he is the potter molding the clay. It was God, the designer of the genetic code, who decided whether you would be a male or a female, tall or short. God has been creating you highly intelligent, or very creative, or a fine mathematician or musician. Or God has been creating you mentally simple, or tense and methodical, or a lover of ordinary routine. A correct relationship with God, therefore, begins in acknowledging everything about you as God's gift. It has to move on then to approving what God has done and is doing in you—even those things that other people might find odd or bad. Acknowledgment, approval, and then thanks: the holy way of the creature in the Creator's hands.

God is the Creator of all public particulars, too, bringing into being and holding in existence all nations—Korean, Czech, Canadian. In the midst of political turmoil, in the quick unfolding of a country's economy, in the gasping development of a global culture, God is making you who you are: calling you to wisdom, and belief in Christ, and hope in the reign of God. The chaos roars around you, and the pandemonium makes it extraordinarily difficult to remember God continually creating you. You will not remember without the help of the church and steady prayer.

The Principle and Foundation

The great spiritual traditions presented Christian life and holiness always in view of eternal life. This was our "final end," and appreciating its eternity and gravity, we decided how to live, what to do, and what not to do. In any choice, however unimportant, we were to ask, "Quid hoc ad eternitatem"—how does this lead to eternal life? Every one of us had the same final end, and we knew that we had to do or avoid the same things. However, God also had a vocation to give to each of us.

Well into modern times, followers felt keenly the stability of the divine order that ordained everything in our lives to lead to eternal life. So we kept the commandments and observed the disciplines of the church. We avoided mortal sins, which were well defined, and practiced virtues in order to save our souls. We understood that a mature person already had a whole soul to save or lose. If we did not follow our vocation, we risked losing our soul; if we followed our vocation faithfully, our soul would be saved by our Redeemer. "What gain, then, is it for a man to have won the whole world and to have lost or ruined his very self?" (Luke 9:25).

With the slow turn to belief in evolution, this solid way has been modified. For we now see the evolution of everything in the world, from earth's vast weather systems to the body's tiny viruses. We see human society evolving, hopefully away from despotism to reasonable freedom. Most important to spirituality, we now see the human self as evolving. We are not complete before death. We are coming to be, day by day, an evolving self.

One result of this change in understanding is that we are not so sure how we can know God's will for us. In the past, we had the sense that God gave each of us a vocation to follow to our final end, eternal life. But how can God assign a vocation to a creature who somehow comes to be precisely by its own free choices? However we look at it, we find it difficult to talk clearly about God's will. Yet God is God, infinite and all-powerful, whether we are modern or anything else.

Perhaps we need a further shift in perspective. From our viewpoint, a vocation functions at the beginning of a life and a final end at its termination. God sees things rather differently. For in God, there is neither yesterday nor tomorrow; everything is now. So we can understand that our Creator hopes that at the end of our lives we will have become what God means us to be at the beginning. Assigning us our final end, God is also assigning us our original purpose.

Every creature has a unique original purpose. From one kind of seed grows a rose and not an oak; from one fertilized egg, a bald eagle and not a bear. In everything that comes into being, there is purpose and tendency so steady that scientists talk about "the laws of nature" and rely on them absolutely. Two atoms of hydrogen and one of oxygen, unless something prevents it, will become a molecule of water every time. Some scientists suggest that from the instant of the big bang (if that is where creation started), all the matter that we know as earth was endowed with an original purpose: to evolve into human life. By now, some say, humans are the last creatures on the globe evolving according to their original purpose. (If only more of us grasped it and lived it!)

Just by being of the earth, then, each of us has a unique original purpose. But God is also creating each of us directly, so it is God who puts into each of us a unique original purpose. We each have a personal vocation from God. No one else can do what God calls each one of us to do, for evolution careens on through time and space.

You are unique and unrepeatable—well, what are you for? Who are you to become? These are questions of more than personal importance, for God's hopes for the world depend on your realizing God's hopes in you.

God's Passionately Creative Desiring

Jesus of Nazareth said more than once that he did only what he felt the Father giving him to do, nothing different and nothing else. "For the Father loves the Son and shows him everything he does himself, and he will show him even greater things than these, works that will astonish you" (John 5:20). How did Jesus come to know what the Father wanted? "My food," he said, "is to do the will of the one who sent me, and to complete his work" (John 4:34). How did Jesus know what "his work" was?

First of all, he knew by being completely open to the revelation given to the people of God. When he was a boy, his parents found him "sitting among the doctors, listening to them, and asking them questions" (Luke 2:46). Once he was mature, he listened not uncritically, but still with great fidelity. Jesus was describing himself when he said, "The man who keeps them [the law and the prophets] and teaches them will be considered great in the kingdom of heaven" (Matthew 5:19).

If we intend to walk his way, we also need to be open to what the Holy Spirit is now revealing in and through the people of God, the church. We attend to the church not uncritically, but not disdainfully or carelessly, either. Jesus watched every jot and tittle. It does not seem to be a bad idea for those who follow him to heed at least the broad strokes.

To know what the Father wanted, Jesus had to make up his own mind about a lot of controverted issues. Should the people of God keep the Sabbath as rigidly as the Pharisees required of themselves? Should the people believe that the dead rise, contrary to the teaching of the Sadducees? Should the people pay taxes to their pagan oppressors? Jesus had to come to his own convictions, just as each one of us must.

How then did Jesus know what the Father wanted him to believe and to preach? He knew by knowing what he himself chose to believe and preach. His long prayers were surely a means of sifting through possibilities and choosing his way. He could trust his desires because he knew that his relationship with the Father was one of perfect trust, absolute obedience, and passionate love. He could trust his own desiring even to the point of begging the Father to take the cross away from him.

This is how we try to know what God wants in us: we grow into Jesus' relationship with the Father, trusting God absolutely, wanting only what God wants, and loving God with our whole heart and strength. Then we let the Holy Spirit teach us what we most authentically desire.

There is a deep truth here. Desiring is at the core of our selves; we feel desires in the present, and out of them we make the future. More, God the Lord creates even the desires of each human being. What each of us wants rises out of the passionately creative love of God. Our God *wants* and wants infinitely. In calling us to life, God shares that desiring with us. He shares first of all the desire to love the infinitely lovable God, and, because we are many, he then shares among all of us his love for each of us.

Here is our ultimate intimacy with our Creator: even our most intimate desires rise in and from God. Why do this man and this woman desire only each other? Because God is raising the desire in each of them. What makes a woman desire to sculpt or a man to create a business? Because, unless sin has skewed their desiring, God's love is raising these desires in them.

Here is the rule for finding the God who is acting in the world: do what God wants, and want what God does. By finding in our selves and our life world those desires that rise most directly and purely out of God's passionate desiring, we find what God hopes for. We find, to put it another way, God's will. Ignatian spirituality offers to facilitate this finding. Like every spiritual tradition, it begins with our need to find out how sin has contaminated our desiring.

The Greater Glory of God

We tend to act today as though giving God glory means roping everyone into having spirituality. Spiritual guides have been eager to teach people to pray. Unhappily, we may have been neglecting what the majority of Catholics really want and need: a way of life.

For most Catholics, as far as our experience instructs us, living the Catholic religion fully is enough. That life is so rich that some call it spirituality, though practicing religion differs from living an interior life in one of the spiritual traditions.

In practicing religion, you are rooted in a community of believers and cannot live your faith apart from them. You embrace the truths of revelation by learning what the church teaches. You follow the commandments and pay attention to the established laws of the church. As a mature member, you know perfectly well that you must shape your own conscience and must not allow controversies about sex and politics to disturb your trust and hope in God. You will not manage this for long if you try it without the guidance of pastors and theologians.

The church has a great tradition of prayer and worship, but this is just the beginning of a practice of religion that is truly enough. The church is a community, and a community has its own way of life, its own culture. The Catholic culture, everywhere on earth, has either never adequately evolved or seriously eroded. We need to form a comprehensive Catholic way of life once again: worship, devotions, corporal and spiritual works of mercy. The church now needs not reformation, but re-formation, and that is the first "greater" intended by "the greater glory of God."

There is another way to give greater glory to God, involving an interior life of spirituality. Such a life is given over to service in the church and the world. This is a life that can be called an oblation to God. Though the ways people live such a life are varied, many have chosen for God's sake a way less traveled, the way of celibacy and service in the church or of married life consecrated to witness and service in society. The present pope is singling out many of them for beatification: A doctor who remained single so that he could serve the poor, for Christ's sake. A woman who surrendered a comfortable status to live among the poor and outcast and help them gain their human dignity. A successful young athlete who built up the religion of his peers and died young. A diocesan priest who spent his considerable gifts getting basic education to underprivileged children.

We are afraid today in most places to put the challenge of such a life to ourselves, and particularly to our young. Perhaps part of our fear makes good sense, because not everyone is called to what Jesus called the rich man to do: "Sell all that you own and distribute the money to the poor, and you will have treasure in heaven; then come, follow me" (Luke 18:22). Jesus called only some to do this. He had many followers who were his disciples; he chose only a few to come along with him in his way of celibacy and self-sacrifice.

A few among us feel that call. When we make the long retreat, we come to the end with a great desire to love the way God loves, returning all back to God. We say to God, "Give me only your love and your grace; that's enough for me."

Not many are called to this way of spirituality. But every single disciple of Christ is called to declare from where God places him or her, "Give me only your love and your grace; it's enough for me."

Contemplative in Action

Jesus of Nazareth leapt from the bosom of the Father into the womb of the lady Mary, a womb such as the one that nurtured each of us. He was incarnate in the same human nature as we are, given as much to violence as to harmony. He lived in an occupied country whose religious leaders were vehemently divided. He had to deal with the spite of enemies and the failure of friends. He gathered disciples, both men and women, to live the true life of the covenant.

In the recent past, and in some places still today, the church has emphasized that Jesus is the Christ, the One in whom resides the fullness of divinity. But Jesus of Nazareth is also the visible image of the invisible God, the Son of Man. In him resides the fullness of humanity. His human life showed how any human who fully accepts being a child of God will live. He is the firstborn, who by full obedience to God ended the slavery of humanity to sin and death.

Every Christian spirituality draws a person to Jesus of Nazareth, who became the Christ. Each spirituality does so in its own way. Ignatian spirituality calls on you to enter into the life of Jesus and, putting on his mind and adopting his purposes, continue his project of building a kingdom of justice and peace in your own day and place.

When you make the Spiritual Exercises, the originating experience of Ignatian spirituality, you pray from the very beginning to know Jesus your Savior. You end your first hour of prayer by addressing Jesus as he hangs on his cross. For three of the four Weeks, you beg God at the beginning of every one of the five daily hours of prayer for the grace to know Jesus better, to love him more, and to follow him more closely.

You are asking more than an interior personal grace, first of all because Jesus lived in close relationship with those whom God gave him to love and be loved by and even with those who chose to resist him. To know and love Jesus entails knowing and loving those whom God puts around you, as Jesus had to do, including even those who hurt you.

This excellent knowledge of the Lord reaches beyond understanding and even beyond feelings. This way of knowing affects your whole self—feelings, judgments, desirings, doings. For as the Holy Spirit reveals to you more and more who Jesus is, the Spirit reveals more and more who you are. You cannot really know Jesus of Nazareth without realizing that God your Creator is making you, too, a chosen one. That same Spirit who shaped Jesus of Nazareth—the boy who grew in wisdom and age and grace, the man who left home to preach, the prophet who was executed—now teaches you how to live as one chosen and precious to the Father.

It works this way: The more we accept knowing Jesus of Nazareth, the more we love him. The more we love him, the more freely we enter into his heart and mind. The Spirit can reveal to those who allow it how Jesus felt about his fate and what passionate desires moved him in his public life. Then we are free to let the Spirit show us what we asked at the beginning of each hour of contemplation: how to go where he went. Led by his Spirit, we grow meek and humble of heart even when battling principalities and powers, as the Lord did. We grasp and try to fulfill his purposes. For the more like Jesus of Nazareth the Spirit makes us, the better we know what he hopes for us and for his earthly kingdom. Having put on the mind of Christ, continually embracing it in prayer and reflection, we now know what to do in order to bring the kingdom to our time and place. This is following Christ as a contemplative in action.

10

God's Project

If spirituality is taken as a strictly personal endeavor, the Spiritual Exercises come across as individualistic and Ignatian spirituality seems to be a matter of prayer and personal relationship with God. But spirituality as the church has always understood it deals with much more than just a person's individual life. Spirituality leads us to know what God wishes in us, which is that we contribute uniquely to the building of the kingdom. We are sent: "As the Father sent me, so am I sending you" (John 20:21).

This is God's plan. We find deep truth in the saints' insistence on it. As rain falls and causes seeds to grow, "so the word that goes from my mouth does not return to me empty, without carrying out my will and succeeding in what it was sent to do" (Isaiah 55:11). The church has always known that God has a plan for all humankind and for each person. Theologians have proclaimed that this plan exists in eternity, since God orders all things sweetly from end to end. Centuries ago, no one grasped how things evolve; nature and grace were thought to be fixed. We cannot now ignore change. We still see magnificent design in all creation; scientists in particular depend on it. This is God's plan.

We know, happily, that God has chosen to evolve creation, to bring it to be moment by moment. From our viewpoint, even the design is unfolding. We know that the earth is constantly shifting and unfolding. We are keenly aware that each individual comes to be a full person only through many truly free choices. Where does God's fixed plan fit in this world?

When we talk about a plan, we have in mind the image of a blueprint, something fully designed and unalterable. But a plan also has to be worked out in the concrete, and in that it becomes a project. It might be helpful, as we stress God's working in the concrete world, to talk about God's project.

Why "God's project"? God creates among all creatures some who can share the divine freedom. In them, by his Holy Spirit, God inspires dreams and desires for a world of justice, peace, and love. From all humankind, God also elects some to know more fully "the mystery of his purpose, the hidden plan he so kindly made in Christ from the beginning to act upon when the times had run their course to the end" (Ephesians 1:9–10). This is a tremendous responsibility, given to those "chosen from the beginning, under the predetermined plan of the one who guides all things as he decides by his own will" (Ephesians 1:11). Here is a truth that not everyone can grasp: we are God's project for our world. We dream and desire under the guidance of the Spirit and are co-creators even of God's reign.

Hence, the original purpose that God breathes in us when he calls us by our name in our mothers' wombs—our personal vocation—is indeed ours and for us. But each one of our vocations is also meant to shape the world. Creating each one of us moment by moment, God raises in us, out of the divine passionate love, those desires that will shape not only each person's individual life but also the life of all of us together and even the physical world. "Be fruitful, multiply, fill the earth and conquer it" (Genesis 1:28).

We who know Jesus Christ in the church will discover a good deal about our personal vocation within the church. It gives good guidelines, both positive and negative. For instance, the church declares positively that, barring extraordinary errors of judgment, you are free to let your marriage shape you profoundly as a person. Following the church, you can contribute well to the reign of God in a conventional life in your culture. It may be, however, that you are called to something more by the Spirit; then you will expect to find that your personal vocation calls you beyond the approved conventional life in your world.

We are free, it has to be said, to be co-creators of another reign: the reign of evil. When we do what God hopes for, we are sharing God's infinite goodness. When we do what God could never approve, God is still creating us in our doing, even when we are freely destroying our self and, in some greater or lesser measure, our life world. This insult offends the good God and is what we mean by sin. What the faithful friend of Jesus Christ wants more than anything, therefore, is to know what God is doing in this moment in order to do that freely, too. The faithful friend does what God wants and wants what God is doing.

Responsibility for Desires

A serious interior life reaches even into our desiring. We want to put and keep some order in our desiring so that we know which desires come from God and which come from somewhere else. We examine our conscience and pray not merely to name and repent of sin, but also to name and own our truest desires. This leads to a self-knowledge that differs from what psychiatry and social psychology can teach us, fine as that is. It brings us to an appreciation of our core self as responsible not only for our actions but even for our desiring, since our desiring expresses God's hopes for us and our life world.

Perhaps we should say that our desiring *can* express God's hopes, for some desires may express hopes other than God's. The reason is this: all of us learn to desire under the influence of others. Teenagers in Tokyo want to listen to hard rock. Why? This year, everyone is reading some best seller. Why? People absorb advertising in the media and come to want things they may never have thought of before. Why is advertising so successful? What makes us want things for ourselves that "everyone has"? Each person's desire is, in large measure, influenced by others.

We desire to do evil things for much the same reason we desire to do good: the influence of others. Some concrete cases are infamous: Drug pushers inveigle the young into using drugs and then pushing them among their peers. Businesspeople solicit immoral collaboration by feeding the lust for lots of money. Pimps promote prostitutes. Parents endure incest. But in everyday life, every one of us shares in this problem. For every culture inculcates evil perspectives, values, desires, and habits. We grow, for instance, to a genuine disdain for some classes in our culture. We embrace hatred for our nations' enemies.

This pervasive influence on our desiring has consequences when we come to ask the Lord to reveal to us our personal vocation. The desiring of others and the structure of desire in our cultures make it difficult for us to discern what our personal vocation might be. This is why, in the church, we "give encouragement to each other, and keep strengthening one another" (1 Thessalonians 5:11). We attend to the lives of the saints and listen to the manifestly good people in our life world. The present Holy Father understands this well and has been declaring many laymen and laywomen and religious and priests safe influences on our desiring.

More securely than in any other way, however, those who are called to an interior life will learn their authentic desiring by contemplating the life of Jesus of Nazareth. All of us who are baptized can trust that our desire to follow the commandments and the disciplines of the church is authentic. That is, if we follow it, we will become the unique, unrepeatable person God longs for and will also be making the kingdom come. Those of us who feel called by the Spirit to something more find that we must sift out from all the things we desire, from all possible ambitions and plans, those desires that rise most directly out of the passionately creative love of God.

How do you take responsibility for a desire? First of all, obviously, you decide whether to follow it or not. If you begin to want someone as an intimate friend, you decide to spend more time with that person. If you want to compete as an athlete, you start to train. If you want to know Jesus Christ, you read Scripture and pray.

How do we know which desires in us rise from God's passionately creative love? Negatively, we know that any desire that leads to sin cannot come from God. We would, moreover, at least distrust any desire that just *might* lead me or someone else to sin—we just distrust and weigh it carefully, as we would before leaving a pile of cash on a desk in a shadowy, much-trafficked room.

Positively, every desire rising out of God's infinite love leads to love—love of God, of neighbor, and of self. A desire that is holy enacts love, making me more loving and inviting others to be the same. Furthermore, we can expect such a desire to enact and enhance the gifts given us by the Holy Spirit in baptism: love, joy, peace, patience, goodness and kindness, trustfulness, gentleness, and self-control. In brief, "whatever you say or do" (or refuse to do, or want to do), "let it be in the name of the Lord Jesus" (Colossians 3:17).

12

What Jesus of Nazareth Wanted

Jesus of Nazareth had to sift out of his desiring the ambitions and misjudgments of his life world. His work at that gives us a model, one that the Spiritual Exercises pursues in many hours of prayer. St. Anselm believed that the Son came into our flesh to do an infinite act of reparation. Whatever the truth of that, Jesus did something considerably closer to our experience: he grew into human freedom in a way infinitely pleasing to God. What makes us pray to follow Jesus of Nazareth is that he grew into a mature person whom we can understand and imitate.

Jesus grew up amid cultural confusion, entertaining some notions that seem strange to us today (the heavens are a solid dome, the earth stands on stilts in the deep). Moreover, he grew up in the chaos of an occupied country plagued by sporadic rebellions hatched in a history of violence. The religious leaders of his day divided not only on politics but also on the most serious religious issues.

How did Jesus grow? St. Paul later gave an important clue: "With him it was always Yes" (2 Corinthians 1:19). As all of us must, Jesus had first of all to approve of the real world and the real people whom God the Father had given him. Jesus' human nature was not created just so that he might become a poor citizen of an occupied nation. Jesus of Nazareth was sent from God's side to be poor in every way—to perceive the sky as a dome, to live in an occupied and repressed nation, to suffer from dodgy religious teachers and cynical political leaders—and Jesus of Nazareth quietly accepted all these kinds of poverty. Through it all, Jesus sought out and accepted what was good, even though it was limited and imperfect. Jesus' *yes* rose from his spirit both wholly resolute and exquisitely nuanced. His disciples today need to follow him in this.

As he grew in age, he had to find what he wanted and then choose whether or not to do it. He felt social pressure to marry, without doubt. What did he want? He learned in his choice of celibacy that there are eunuchs made that way for the kingdom. He had to decide early on whether to study the law. As a twelve-year-old, he had wanted to learn in the temple. Governed by St. Joseph and the lady Mary, he abandoned that boyish ambition. But then, more adult, he had to decide how far he wanted to follow John the Baptist, whom he admired almost extravagantly, believing that "of all the children born of women, there is no one greater than John" (Luke 7:28).

He chose to believe in the resurrection of the body. With the scribes, he agreed entirely about keeping every jot and tittle of the law. But from a youth readily hearing and obeying, he grew to a mature religious man who wanted to know the real law, refusing to judge "according to appearances," but only according to what is right (John 7:24). He learned that even good people live for the approval of others, "not concerned with the approval that comes from the one God" (John 5:44).

His decisions touched on politics and civil order as well as religion. Challenged, he gave his opinion that Jews should pay the taxes extorted by the Roman occupiers: "Give back to Caesar what belongs to Caesar—and to God what belongs to God" (Luke 20:25). He came to value and to want to help pagan Roman officials who felt trust in his work. He decided, after a conversation with a woman at a well, that Samaritans as well as Israelites could approach the kingdom. He came to appreciate that the true law demands that everyone, even the most despised outcast, is to be treated as a neighbor.

The core of his desiring was religious. He wanted to announce the Good News, drawing the people back to a faithful observance of the covenant. But over time, he came to see that doing the teaching he wanted to do would put him into dangerous opposition with the religious authorities. Did he want to go that far? He grew in his conviction to the point of telling his enemies, "When you have lifted up the Son of Man, then you will know that I am He and that I do nothing of myself: What the Father has taught me is what I preach" (John 8:28).

13

From the Time of Adam

We do not like to think about sin. This is understandable first of all because sin is a mystery. We can understand it only by pondering what has been revealed to us. This is not easy to think about, either: sin destroys what God wishes for humankind and for each person, and we are the destroyers. When we live an interior life, we confront our own sin over and over. Here lies another reason why we do not like to think about sin: it is not a problem we can solve. It is a force that we need to be saved from.

Start with how completely sin has corrupted some persons. The first place goes to Lucifer. Jesus said, "I watched Satan fall like lightning from heaven" (Luke 10:18). In the theology of Master Ignatius's day, the angels had one chance to say yes or no to God's will. Lucifer said no. You don't have to be a rocket scientist to get the point: sin can corrupt totally.

We so dislike thinking that sin destroys the self that we have trouble believing in hell. We prefer to believe that truly vicious acts must be the result of psychic disorders; they cannot be rationally chosen. A man murders several people and we exclaim, "Oh, that is sick." Persons who murder little children must surely be insane. Well, yes, perhaps they are. How did they get that way? Our presumption is that they are that way because of their childhood or some wrong wrinkle in the cortex of their brain.

The presumption gets in the way of our seeing a terrible truth: it is possible for any one of us to make ourselves insane by repeatedly choosing to do evil things. It is a profoundly evil thing to drive into insanity a self whom God our Creator and Lord cherishes.

We are surrounded by people who do that. We may not judge their subjective guilt; God is their judge. But we must judge the lives they lead. We must judge the kind of choices they make that lead to sinful insanity. Otherwise, we have effectively denied human freedom—ironically, pretending that true freedom cannot possibly lead to death.

Here is what Jesus of Nazareth said about seeing and not seeing sin: "It is for judgement that I have come into this world, so that those without sight may see and those with sight turn blind" (John 9:39). The religious professionals in Jesus' life saw the same things that Jesus saw. But they refused to judge correctly. A lot of fairly good disciples of Jesus do the same thing today. It is a serious mistake.

Reflect on people in your own life world who have chosen manifestly evil lives. You can follow them on their way. Over and over again, you can choose to lie, and soon you will be a liar. You know who the father of lies is. You can repeatedly steal from the business you work for, and you will become a thief. You can act violently in anger, and in not many years you will be a raging maniac. "The wicked man's oracle is Sin in the depths of his heart" (Psalm 36:1). And from that evil heart comes all kinds of evil in its life world. Evil heart links to evil heart, and they create the "structures of sin." So the structures of sin are not impersonal, like the force of gravity. The injustices and oppressions rife in the world today are the result of collusion of people who are free to do other than they do.

Refuse to let the revelation of the mystery of sin penetrate your spirit, and you will not fully appreciate the mystery of God's merciful love for you. "What proves that God loves us is that Christ died for us while we were still sinners" (Romans 5:8). If we think we are just mistaken or incomplete or need medication, we will never feel the weight of that proof of God's love.

Every one of us has chosen to sin at some time: "If we say we have no sin in us, we are deceiving ourselves and refusing to admit the truth" (1 John 1:8). The spiritual life that does not confront sin honestly and repeatedly is built on sand.

Conversation by the Cross

All the great spiritual traditions refer to a conversation with God at the end of a time of prayer. Ignatian spirituality urges making such a "colloquy." During your prayer, you might be thinking of the Father or of Jesus in the third person, as "he," even while remaining in the holy presence. You reflect about Jesus, "He enjoyed being with people," or about God the Father, "He is greater than all created things combined." But prayer is a conversation, so sooner or later you will address God as "you." You will speak to Jesus as to a friend or your Redeemer; you will speak to God as to a tender Master who holds you in the palm of his hand.

You may already in your prayer have been speaking directly to the Father or to Jesus Christ—or to one of those whom Jesus of Nazareth loved, such as the lady Mary or St. Peter. But speaking your heart to God at the end of your prayer is a good practice. And you will move along in an Ignatian spiritual practice more surely if you take a moment at the end of your prayer time to look back over what you have experienced and choose what you want to say to the Lord. The practice may seem a bit artificial, but it is actually an act of reverence. Who would not prepare what to say before going to talk to a country's ruler? The pause also shows reverence for yourself; it reminds you that God hopes you will approach him as you are, in full freedom.

No one can tell you what you ought to say, obviously, as these matters are between you and God. Saints adept at prayer, however, have sometimes spelled out for their disciples the things they might want to say. St. Francis de Sales, for instance, suggests a lot of holy aspirations and petitions. And when Master Ignatius gave the full Exercises, he sometimes suggested prayers that he had composed as "colloquies" after two of the meditations. He incorporated these brief texts into the book of the Spiritual Exercises. The first comes at the end of the first hour of prayer, during which you ponder the sin of the angels, the sin of Adam and Eve, and how a sin-filled death could finally have destroyed a man even though he had gained the whole world.

If you follow Ignatius's suggestion for the colloquy that follows this hour of prayer, you imagine yourself standing before Jesus on the cross. Then you let a blazing question hover between you and Jesus: How does it happen that you, Lord, are being punished in this ferocious way as an evildoer, when you are no evildoer? How does it happen that I am not punished, when I am an evildoer?

When you ask this with an open heart, you find the revelation you want to cling to when you reflect on sin. You cannot make any sense of the revelation that Jesus of Nazareth is the Son of God, whom "the Father has consecrated and sent into the world" (John 10:36), unless you appreciate that God faithfully loves those whom he creates. He will not let your sin stand between his love and you. As a lover, he freely chose to do what love demanded. "No one takes [my life] from me; I lay it down of my own free will" (John 10:18). So the question comes back to you who are asking Jesus how he came to be on the cross. What have you done for him? What are you doing for him? What might you do for him? In various ways, these three questions recur in the prayer of those who practice Ignatian spirituality in the world today.

15

Redeemer and Redeemed

Imagination is a way of knowing. It frees us to appreciate what rational thought might not help us grasp. Here is a fantasy to help you appreciate that while humankind is powerless over sin, we are not helpless.

Imagine the kind of event that has been happening for millennia all over the world: An infant, filthy and naked, sits on the earth crying in heartbreak, raising his helpless arms and shrieking in frustration. Around him lies the wreckage of a primitive village, its thatch burned to blowing gray ashes and its blackened wood flickering and smoldering. Bodies of adult and young men, gashed, smashed, and broken, lie motionless all around the infant. He is bruised, too, the side of his head swollen yellow and purple where the marauders gave a blow they meant to kill him. They may as well have. He tries to crawl but crumbles.

The sun goes down behind the menacing hills from which the horsemen had thundered and over which they went, dragging women and children. The infant's cries go hoarse as thirst dries him out. He tries again to crawl but falls, toppling over onto the massive bruise disfiguring his forehead. He hiccups, shrieks. Acrid fumes sting his watering eyes and mouth. He gurgles in uncomprehending terror. Dark has come. The last tongues of fire flicker yellow and orange. The infant folds into himself and falls on his side, exhausted, empty. His great, ripened bruise pulses. His little body jerks in sleep.

Dreaming, or feeling truth, he knows a great hand has cradled his head, and another his body. The hands hold him firmly and raise him off the earth. He finds a vague face, hideous behind a russet crust of bloody face hair. It is real. A young man who had been left for dead was only deeply stunned. The infant feels himself held snugly against a hirsute chest. He is swung around and bounced, securely held. He sucks on a rag soaked in sweet water. He feels a great hand wipe from his face the tears and the terror. He sinks into the safe, warm chest and sleeps.

You are that child, and Christ Jesus is that warrior who was wounded to death and lives again. You could put it this way: you are a cry for help. But the fact that you sin is not the deepest truth about you. The deepest truth is that you are powerless before sin. You are powerless to overcome all the disabilities, limitations, and wrongs that fester in you because of sin and, above all, to block the inexorable approach of sin's final act, your death. You truly are as powerless as that infant to get up and heal yourself, to rise from your woundedness and the world's ruin into a mature, whole human person.

At this time, when humankind surely is most conscious of its incessant savagery, you know that God is intensely active, creating you out of concrete chaos. God creates you from nothing, as the faith teaches, which means that nothing in you could force God to call you into existence. God calls because of his love. And in his fidelity, he calls you out of the chaos of your life world to grace. How those who do not know Christ manage not to despair is hard to say. We do not despair because we know that our Redeemer lives. We are powerless, but never helpless. Our Creator has said to each one of us: "I have called you by your name, you are mine" (Isaiah 43:1).

16

Conversion of Heart

Christians tend to take Paul's experience of conversion as the paradigm, as though we all need to be knocked off a horse. Ignatian guides today regularly point to Master Ignatius's conversion as another paradigm. It was dramatic enough: in a matter of months, a vain courtier was led from a life of irresponsible sex and swordplay to one of a mystic given to excesses in fasting and self-abasement. While both Paul's and Ignatius's paradigms are inspiring, neither gives much practical help to a contemplative religious or a busy parent.

Yet we all need to understand conversion, which the church now says should be ongoing. We cannot keep falling off a horse, so whatever can "ongoing conversion" mean? To start with, it means that every one of us keeps on committing sins—in thoughts, words, and deeds. Beyond that, it means that the chaos raging in our cultures also roils our own hearts, and we need to do something about it. And finally, ongoing conversion means that neither sins nor chaos will go away just because we love God. Conversion is not a onetime dramatic instance of being knocked off a horse by God. It is a much humbler, and more humbling, experience.

Conversion begins when we honestly face our sin and disorder and decide to take responsibility for them and for ourselves. The Holy Spirit teaches us (as does our own spirit) that something we are doing or omitting is wrong and invites us to account for it: What is this something about? What does it say about who I am? The matter will be a concrete issue in one of the five areas of our experience: religious, moral, intellectual, affective, and sociopolitical. We experience everything as a whole person, of course, so our experience in any one of these areas affects (negatively or positively) our experience in the others. A moral decision that taxes are hurting the poor changes how we think and act politically. Affection for a foreign people makes it easier to learn their language.

We can be certain that the Spirit will call us to grow day by day. What are some examples of this growth? We become aware that our feelings about the church are everyone else's and decide to shape our own: this is the religious conversion of a maturing Christian. We recognize that our ideas about raising teenagers are vague and not useful, so we make inquiries and read some books: this is the intellectual conversion of a responsible parent. We realize that we have been saying half truths about someone at work and decide to say good things instead: this is the moral conversion of a conscientious colleague. We feel alienated and admit that we have been neglecting dear friends, so we start contacting them: this is an affective conversion of one called to love others. We have to admit that we have done nothing for the hungry and decide to contribute to Bread for the World: this is the sociopolitical conversion of someone called to bring the kingdom.

Jesus faced people who needed these conversions. Nicodemus, for instance, had morality straight but needed intellectual conversion in his understanding of God's revelation. James and John called for violence on those who refused their Master, who drew them to the religious conversion of nonviolence toward enemies. Some lawyers were allowing sons to favor the temple treasury over support of their elderly parents, and Jesus told them that they had better have a moral conversion.

Why we need ongoing conversion becomes clear when we understand that we are God's project for our life world. Patiently, the Holy Spirit shapes us, because our virtues are not for us alone; they are for the world around us. Through the teaching of the church, through prayer on the life of Jesus, through holy friendships, the Spirit of Christ is shaping the kingdom to come. Our conversions may not be as dramatic as those of St. Paul and Master Ignatius. They are nonetheless as truly consequential.

The Examen of Conscience

Master Ignatius urged a regular examination of conscience, and his companions were convinced that after the experience of the Spiritual Exercises, one should continue making the "examen" daily (even twice daily) for the rest of one's life. Ignatian guides today might recommend that you make this brief exercise (perhaps fifteen minutes) at noon and in the evening, though many make it at other times of the day.

The examen is less about our sin than about our growth in Christlife. At any given moment, every living thing is either growing or dying; which are we doing now? Further, the examen focuses mainly on what we do, because our love for God is real when we act on it. Guided by the Spirit, we decide to take responsibility for ourselves in one or more of the five areas of human experience by doing what we need to do to be more fully alive in Christ. This is "making progress," a recurrent phrase in Ignatian spirituality. It is complex enough to require daily attention in the examen.

The Ignatian examen takes its typical form in five moments. The first is thanking God for all good gifts. We might begin with the grandest, such as life and light and the freedom and plenty we live in. But we do well to get to particulars: We kept a decision to pray in the morning. We finished an important project. We resolved a conflict with a colleague or got a note of congratulations from another. It is useful to thank God well, because ingratitude is the root of self-centeredness, and gratitude opens the self to God and others.

The second moment is a prayer for courage to see clearly how things stand between us and God. We need courage because once we have progressed beyond just staying out of sin, we tend to let our gifts stand in the way of our growing in love for Christ. We spend so much time exercising a gift for writing that we seriously neglect those we love. We shower so much affective attention on others that we neglect quiet time with Jesus Christ. When we lead a serious interior life, we need courage to see that we readily choose to do good things that are, too many times, the wrong ones.

After this, the time comes to examine how we have done since last time. Each of us finds our own way to do this. Sometimes we have to look carefully at a single experience: an outburst of anger or a deliberate little lie. We ask, What is this about? Under every such experience lie ideas and convictions that we might not really approve of in ourselves. Another time, finding nothing special, we might focus on patterns of feeling or action that ran through the whole day: an anxiety that kept us hopping from one thing to another, for instance. And finally, we may well try to focus on one concrete issue and look into how we have done in addressing it. For instance, we have decided to take responsibility for being calm and reasonable during a continuing office conflict. How did that go?

It takes awhile to look over our actions and affections while staying present to God our Lord. But a moment comes when we know what we need to say to the Lord. So, fourth, we turn to God our Creator and Lord and speak directly to him about what we have found. We may find God surprising us with insight and consoling us with trust and love. We might have to bring to the Father our weariness with a social habit we cannot shake. We might have to profess to him that we have not lived in hope during these hours. And we need to beg God's mercy.

There is one final moment, the fifth, in which we consider what comes next. It is true that we cannot control the future, but we shape the present by how we envision the future. So we take the time to imagine how well we can do without some unholy habit we have chosen to shake, or how we will grow beyond a prejudice we feel. In this moment, we go back to gratitude. We make sure before God that we will accept whatever changes in ourselves—in any of the realms of human experience—that may happen as we grow in grace, as God wishes us to grow. For God our Creator and Lord is the Master of our lives; we are not.

An Ignatian Framework for Prayer

I s there a specifically Ignatian kind of contemplation? Well, Master Ignatius recommended a characteristic framework for each hour of prayer. He was clear, however, that each person prays as the Lord leads. And in any case, the framework's several elements were common in the church when he was learning how to pray from Benedictines, Carthusians, Dominicans, and others.

The Ignatian framework is simple enough. First, you do well to prepare beforehand the matter you will pray with. This would include having identified a definite event in Jesus' life, or a prayer you intend to pray through, or some other material. If you have made the long retreat, you may take its contemplations as material for daily prayer for a while. If you have made the Exercises in daily life, you may have accepted the suggestion that you pray with the Gospel of the day, praying in that way with the whole church.

Whatever you have chosen, you might decide that there are certain points or particulars you want to attend to during prayer. This even helps when you are entering into an event in Jesus' life and is particularly helpful when you are working on some decision or handling a difficult stretch in your life. If you go to the text of *The Spiritual Exercises*, you will find given with each of the events in Jesus' life three "points" to be considered. You need not worry that you might be standing in the Spirit's way, as the Spirit is greater than your plans.

As you begin your prayer, you first come to self-concentration in God's presence. You do reverence to God, perhaps by kneeling or touching your forehead to the ground or just by standing still. This "act of presence" opens the door to Ignatian prayer by beginning to create its context. The context is completed by begging God that this time of prayer may begin in him and through his Spirit end in his praise and service. As a zendo is the context of Zen meditation and a choir is the context of the prayer of the Hours, this deliberate self-concentration in God's presence and decision to do all in him forms the context of Ignatian prayer.

Where you do this prayer depends on where the Spirit leads you. When you grow accustomed to making mental prayer, you will probably have identified a special place in which to do it. If you are like most people today, it will be a place in a chapel or a chair in your room.

Ignatian spirituality includes some further specific frameworks for each of the different kinds of prayer: fantasy, meditation, and contemplation. Common to all of them, we must be aware, is a struggle with "distractions." A wise contemplative woman once said that there is no such thing as a distraction in prayer, because whatever comes into your mind and heart while you are with God in prayer belongs there. Real distraction—as the word suggests—is anything that draws you out of prayer, erasing your sense of God's presence and weakening your sense of being present to yourself.

The framework of Ignatian prayer ends with a colloquy. You spend a moment deciding what to say to the Lord, and then you say it. And last of all, without fail, you say the prayer that the Lord Jesus taught us, the Our Father.

After you have finished praying, you might take time to look back over what you have experienced. This "review of meditation" is not exactly part of the framework of prayer, but it is useful in much the same way that a diary or a journal is useful. For God our Creator and Lord is always at work in us, raising desires and giving us the grace to act. When we go to prayer, we go as who and what we are now, and a journal helps us keep clear about that. God already knows. If we try to fake it, denying or refusing to see how we are right now, God will probably lose interest in the conversation. We will get tired of the charade, too.

19

Friends in the Lord

Ignatian spirituality has always drawn people into spiritual friendship. The first companions of Master Ignatius called themselves simply "friends in the Lord" before they became the Company of Jesus. Today, one of the common outcomes of the Exercises in daily life is the desire to continue in companionship. In part, perhaps, this has to do with our search for community. But the thirst for friendship also suggests that people are making an important choice between living a life for power and living a life for love.

This is a fundamental choice that every one of us faces as we go through life. Like every fundamental choice, it is easier to name than to describe. Yet we all can recognize people around us, in every vocation, who are living out one of these two options.

When we choose the way of power, we want control over our lives and over everything in them. We want to be the ones who choose what work we do and how much and when. A man drags his family all over creation in order to make a business succeed but has little time for his children or his spouse. A pastor runs his parish like a baron in a fiefdom; a president runs her organization like a barracuda in a school of fish. None of us can claim we are without taint of this option for power. If we can manage nothing else, we demand control over our opinions, refusing to let friends' thoughts influence us and keeping our distance from church teaching.

The way of power has consequences. We tend not to know ourselves at any depth and want to keep it that way. We keep our own counsel, not opening ourselves even to those we love most and not seeking spiritual friendship. We think that we could do better than anyone in authority. Those who choose power do not often experience *lonesomeness*, the sweetly sad feeling of missing those whom you love and can name. They more often experience *loneliness*, the empty feeling of missing someone but not knowing who. The spiritual consequences of this are obvious: it is hard to keep the marriage vows or the vow of celibacy; it is hard to feel quiet hope in the providence of God; it is hard, finally, to imagine that you are not independent of God as you are independent of everyone else. We do not exactly sin in opting for the way of power. But as in a healthy body whose immune system is suppressed, the deadly infection will come along in time.

The way of love differs entirely. To begin with, you choose to live content in the relationships that God has given you. Living these, you put first your relationship with Jesus Christ and try to love his Mystical Body, the sinful church. You are content to be of your ethnic group and of your nation; your love for them moves you to help and improve them. Your humility comes from knowing that you need continuing conversions in order to be a good friend and lover. You allow yourself to be vulnerable, even to take risks, such as leaving undeveloped a fine talent because serving Christ in your vocation requires it. You trust yourself because you trust God, who says in your heart: "You are precious in my eyes, and I love you."

The way of love brings its consequences as well. A hearty spouse of fifty years once asked his wife as they approached a smorgasbord, "What do I want?" It was not only that she knew better than he; it was also that she had his interests closer to her heart than he had. They both knew that, and it worked both ways. Choosing the way of love leads to trusting God our Creator and Lord that far: he knows better than we what is best for us.

The key to a life of power is wealth. Once you have wealth—and it need not be any great amount, either—you find that you can hardly have enough. You crave security, and that craving drives you and brings anxiety and fear. The key to a life of love is humbly acknowledging that everything is a gift. Once you grow well into the way of love, you find that what you have—wealth or poverty, genius or dullness—is enough. And in that, you accept the joy of the Lord.

.... **20** ....

Enough and More
Than Enough

his may sound harsh, but many serious thinkers say it: too few of us find guidance in the moral norms that Jesus enunciated. Yet the church has remembered a lot of them, which, taken together, add up to a rather comprehensive way of life. Jesus did, after all, answer the question, "Good Master, what have I to do to inherit eternal life?" (Luke 18:18).

Jesus had disciples who followed him very closely. He called them to leave everything—father and mother, wife and lands—for the kingdom's sake. He called them, to use an Ignatian term, to the *magis*, a Latin word for "the greater good." He also had many other disciples who remained in the towns or hillsides where God had planted them. Jesus called them to what we can call the *satis*, a Latin word for "the good enough." Neither group could be excused from listening carefully to the strong moral stances Jesus taught, often with a warning about entering, or not entering, into eternal life.

The great discourse in Matthew's Gospel gives a survey of these teachings as held by the early church, who believed with

Jesus that the one "who keeps them and teaches them will be considered great in the kingdom of heaven" (5:19). Consider this norm about a strained relationship: "Leave your offering there before the altar, go and be reconciled with your brother first, and then come back and present your offering" (5:24). And this about swearing: "All you need say is 'Yes' if you mean yes, 'No' if you mean no; anything more than this comes from the evil one" (5:37). And these words about violence and enemies: "If anyone hits you on the right cheek, offer him the other as well" (5:39); "I say this to you: love your enemies and pray for those who persecute you" (5:44). And this about wealth: "Do not store up treasures for yourselves on earth" (6:19). And about food and clothing, your body and your livelihood: "Your heavenly Father knows you need them all. . . . Do not worry" (6:32, 34).

Perhaps we are tempted to think that Jesus of Nazareth was trying to establish a utopia. Quite a few of the commands he left seem utopian—for instance, the one that we are to "love one another" just as he has loved us (John 13:34). They probably seem utopian because they completely go against human culture and even merely human wisdom. Who hasn't better "sense" than to turn the other cheek? Who can sensibly live without insurance?

A utopia is nowhere and outside of time. Jesus was talking about the here and now. What he commanded transcends mere human wisdom, and to consider it utopian is to remain resolutely bound by mere human wisdom. He insisted on accepting things as God has so far created them and your place in them. "Set your hearts on his kingdom first, and on his righteousness, and all these other things will be given you as well" (Matthew 6:33). Jesus did not say that accepting what we find means acquiescing in what we find—not when what we find is unjust, unholy, unloving. Jesus' way of thinking is fairly direct: See what you see, then see what can be made better and make it better.

The truth is that we may have "spiritualized" the way too far, convinced that praying a lot (and "well") is enough. It is not. Besides instructing all of those who followed him to "be compassionate as your Father is compassionate," he also told them, "Give, and there will be gifts for you . . . the amount you measure out is the amount you will be given back" (Luke 6:36, 38). Today we nervously fear that any close observance of commands must be too mincing and mechanical. Jesus repeatedly insisted that we are to observe "the weightier matters of the Law—justice, mercy, good faith." These, however, we are to practice "without neglecting the others," the pedestrian, everyday duties (Matthew 23:23).

Every one of us knows God's mercy and love. We might just take these into our own rooms and pray in silence, but how Jesus dealt with the Gerasene demoniac occasions another instruction. The man wanted to be a close disciple, but Jesus would not allow it. "'Go back home,' he said 'and report all that God has done for you'" (Luke 8:39). Certainly, some of Jesus' current disciples are summoned to spend their lives proclaiming the Good News. All of us are to tell what God has done and is doing for us.

Ways of Praying

Jesus' command was quite simple: "Pray continually and never lose heart" (Luke 18:1). The way the early church remembered the matter, he was talking more about mundane needs than heavenly truths. As Luke recounts it, Jesus mentioned the command as part of the parable of the unjust judge and the persistent widow. Luke follows this with Jesus' comparison of two visitors to the temple: the proud Pharisee who speaks of how good he is and the humble tax collector who begs God's mercy because he is a sinner.

It is useful to note this here because Ignatian guides today seem to take Jesus' command as a mandate to practice mental prayer—consideration, meditation, and contemplation. That would be mistaken for two reasons. First, Master Ignatius alluded to just about every way of praying in his text and did not direct the one praying to any particular way. Second, some of us are called to practice regular mental prayer and some of us are not—but we are all still obeying Jesus' command by praying in our way.

How you pray is quite literally between you and God. But it is important to notice that Jesus endowed the church with a rich variety of prayer. Praying the breviary, for instance, keeps your spirit open to the whole range of spiritual experience: praising God and thanking him, complaining about hardships and lamenting society's evils. In praying the psalms, you beg God for his continued care and help, the core of praying continually.

Some of the church's treasured prayers are official, preserved in the Scriptures or the liturgy; many are the shared graces of seriously prayerful men and women. Like Fra Angelico's fresco of the Annunciation and Michelangelo's *Pietà*, those shared graces still move us deeply. Most of us who take prayer seriously come across prayers that linger in this way.

Master Ignatius recommended several ways of praying simply in everyday life. In one, you recall that you live in the presence of the Lord and offer to him all that you do—how else would you start to pray?—and then you slowly recite the creed or the Our Father. Master Ignatius suggests two ways of praying the Our Father. One is to take the prayer word by word. When you are done thinking about one word, you go to the next, and so on. The other way is to recite the Our Father rhythmically, saying one word on each foot as you walk or in each breath as you sit or lie still. You can do this with the Hail Mary and other prayers, too.

As Master Ignatius discovered, some thoughtful people want simple ways to pray mentally. He suggests taking each of the commandments and pondering what it might mean in your life now and how well you are honoring it. You can do the same with the capital sins (pride, greed, lust, envy, anger, gluttony, and sloth), or you can ask how you are serving God and others with your memory, your understanding, your freedom, and your five senses (sight, hearing, smell, taste, and touch). A good practice today is to do the same with any of the many lists developed by psychologists and social engineers: the Enneagram, the seven best practices of an effective manager, and the like. Why not think about how we are calling on our human skills to love God better?

Master Ignatius left us almost none of his own prayers. But one has become a hallmark of Ignatian spirituality. It is called the Suscipe, from its Latin first word, which means "accept." Here is a way to pray it:

> Accept, O Lord, and treat as your own
> my liberty, my understanding,
> my memory—all of my decisions and my freedom to
> choose.
> All that I am and all that I have
> you gave me and give to start;
> now I turn and return all to you,
> looking to find your hopes and will in all.
> Keep giving me your holy love,
> hold on me your life-giving gaze,
> and I neither need nor want anything else.

These simple ways of entering into prayer are particularly helpful when we are tired or distracted. It seems that most people find these ways enough to keep them making progress. Guides are mistaken to try to lead into more formal mental prayer those whom God has chosen to converse with in other ways. Jesus said, "Pray continually." He did not say, "Pray well," and much less, "Pray better."

22

The Prayer of Consideration

Pilots learn many procedures to make flying safe. Doctors learn many ways of dealing with an illness so they can apply the appropriate method to each sufferer. Even tennis players and footballers learn many strategies in order to play well and win. Why would we who want to pray not have our own methods that we can apply appropriately? In making the Spiritual Exercises and living an interior life with Ignatian spirituality, there are three important ways of praying.

The first is the prayer of consideration. This is what Jesus of Nazareth urged his disciples to do when he invited them to "consider the lilies of the field." He was not asking them to puzzle out some botanical conundrum about lilies. He was asking them to turn their minds to the simple facts about the little red flowers growing in the stony field and to let their hearts grasp what flowers and field told them about the love of God their Creator and Lord.

You can pray this way with a Gospel text or a passage from St. Paul. Take the prologue of the Gospel of St. John, for instance.

Coming into God's presence and offering to him all that you now experience, you ponder what it can mean that God has been choosing in eternity to send the Son into our flesh. What has this meant to the history of humankind? What does it mean to your own life world? You ask who, what, when, why, and how.

Or you can take one of Jesus' parables and pray over it less as a story than as a text to interpret, perhaps with some help from Scripture scholars. Take, for example, the story of the prodigal. We always think of the son as the prodigal, which is hardly a wild guess. But the father is prodigal, too, in another sense, just the sense that Jesus intended: he gives and gives and shares all that he has with those whom he loves. What kind of person was the elder son? What made the father so patient with both of his sons? In considering this, you come to a deeper appreciation of the One about whom Jesus told the story. Not the son, but the Father.

This way of praying does not depend on using a text. The lady Mary, for instance, after the experiences she and Joseph had with the child Jesus in the temple, "pondered all these things in her heart." The prayer of consideration is what happens when a mother sits staring into the middle distance wondering what God would have her do about her child. It goes on when a pastor pauses to worry before the Blessed Sacrament about what to do for the faltering lives in his parish. Or when a lawyer asks the Lord about overwork.

Consideration is a readily available way of praying continually, almost an instinctive activity of those who live devout interior lives in a busy world. For instance: you teach, and every day before your students arrive, you sit and ponder what you are doing for them and what you are going to tell them, and you ask God for help. Another instance: you travel to work on a commuter train and sit musing on the relationships among the people closest to you, asking the help of the One who is also Three. Another instance: you read in the Sunday newspaper that the pontiff has spoken out again against violence and war, and you wonder what you think and ask God for peace.

Always as you begin to consider, you remember that God is attending to you, even if you are not attending to God. Offer him your time; then, in the few seconds before you have to break off, remember among your reflections things that you could bring to the Lord. Speak your heart out to the Lord, praying.

The prayer of consideration is serious prayer. We apply all our gifts in this form of prayer, leading off with the gifts of wisdom and understanding. We can note that this prayer seems extraordinarily helpful to those who lead busy lives and that it is the fundamental prayer in Ignatian discernment.

23

The Prayer Called Meditation

Meditation is a way of coming to know Jesus Christ by remembering an event in his life. You recall it in great detail and in exact sequence to begin with, as you might some incident that you actually witnessed. Suppose that you were looking out your window when an accident happened on your street. An automobile ran into a bicycle, and the cyclist was terribly hurt. He was crushed beneath his bike, and there was a lot of blood. You watched as passersby helped get him out from under his bike. You heard him scream when they moved his broken leg. Then you went down to the street.

Now suppose that the police come to investigate and asked everyone standing there to tell what they saw. Who did what? Was there fault involved? You have some time to remember and go over the sequence of events in your mind, and you try to interpret the actions and responsibilities. Then it is your turn to tell. As you go through the event again and again, you feel more and more a part of it. Later on, you tell it to friends almost as though you were part of the incident. What you do in remembering the event, going over its sequence, and interpreting it is the same thing you do in meditating on the life of Jesus.

For instance, you might take the story of the man born blind in John's ninth chapter. You would read through it beforehand, perhaps identifying certain events that you want to concentrate on: Jesus goes and finds the man, the man tells the rulers that Jesus must surely be a prophet, and Jesus goes and finds him again. When you come to meditate, you follow another Ignatian frame of prayer: you remember where the event fits in Jesus' story, you let your imagination re-create the scene, and you pray for the grace to know Jesus of Nazareth better, to love him more, and to follow the way he followed. You say this prayer constantly during the Spiritual Exercises, and no one can live Ignatian spirituality without saying something like it every day.

After you have prepared yourself to pray, you may do something like the following: You picture Jesus going along the wall to a gate. You hear him ask the blind man whether he wishes to be healed. You watch the man go off exulting; he is seeing for the first time in his life. You might wonder what it is like to see trees and stones and other people for the first time—what joys, what puzzlement, what thankfulness? You might ponder the fact that Jesus seemed always to ask: What do you want? And then you might reflect on how God deals with you so courteously and, with almost infinite patience, respects your freedom. And so on. Always in Ignatian prayer, you pause at the end and consider what you want to say to Jesus or the Father. After you have talked with the Lord as a friend or a good servant, you end with the Our Father.

We meditate this way on Jesus' life to bring his experiences into contact with our own. In a certain way, we are asking to stand in Jesus' sandals, though he hasn't taken them off. The fathers of the church referred to this as finding the "spiritual meaning" of the Scriptures. In some ways, praying in this way turns the Scriptures into texts to learn from with our hearts, and not just stories to hear with our ears.

Take the story of the coming of the risen Jesus Christ to his friends when they were fishing off the shore of Lake Galilee. He called to them, and suddenly they recognized him: "It is the Lord" (John 21:7). Peter grabbed his garments, dove into the water, and came dripping up the shore. Peter knew Jesus better now because Peter knew that he was forgiven and that the love between them was stronger than ever. Peter loved Jesus with his wounded passion, and he just wanted to be where Jesus was. That's what Ignatian meditation leads to.

Ignatian Contemplation

Contemplating events in Jesus' life for five hours spread through each day is the main activity of three of the four Weeks in the experience of the Spiritual Exercises. This kind of prayer opens our hearts to God's hopes by letting us enter into the human life of the Son of God. This is crucial, because Jesus' life is our ideal, not in the sense that we will live as he lived, but in the sense that the way he lived gives us a measure of how well we are living. Contemplating his life is the way in which we can best grasp the full implication of our personal vocation, particularly if it is to risk everything for the sake of the kingdom.

Contemplation as a way of praying is part of all the church's great spiritual traditions. In the Carmelite tradition, it leads to a kind of union with God beyond human powers. God sometimes "infuses" a human spirit with a knowing and appreciating that purifies it and unites it to the Holy Trinity in a deeply passionate love.

Contemplation in the Ignatian tradition draws on other parts of the church's spiritual tradition—on the Benedictine *Ejercitatorio Espiritual*, for instance, which divides the reform of life into four "weeks," and on Ludolph of Saxony's great life of Jesus, which puts you right into the events of Jesus' life. We enter into Ignatian contemplation by deliberately applying our human powers of memory, understanding, and will. Each time we pray, we prepare as usual, coming into God's presence and offering the time back to the God who gives it to us. Then we enter into an event in the life of Jesus of Nazareth, using the text of the Scripture passage if that is helpful.

We are not just viewing externals. We ask to enter into Jesus' deepest feelings and desires. We ask, "Lord, you were just a little boy—what made you remain behind in the temple?" Or, "Do you look on me with the same love you felt when you looked on the rich young man?" We rather boldly feel Jesus' anger when he snapped at Peter, "Get behind me, Satan" (Mark 8:33). We ask to enter into Jesus' heart and mind with profound reverence and humility, or else we will not do it much or for long.

When you are making a daily contemplation, and also when you are making the Exercises, you might be helped by an Ignatian method for entering into an event. You first note each person involved. Then you listen to each thing that is said. And finally, you note what each person does. All along, you are reflecting on yourself. You do not merely imagine the event as though you were watching it on film. You enter into the scene, letting it unfold as though you were part of it, standing warm in the temple or ankle-deep in the water of the Jordan. Master Ignatius found it helpful to be a little boy serving Joseph and Mary as they traveled toward Bethlehem. When Ignatius discovered that this helped others, too, he included it in his text.

The experience of contemplation is often vivid and real. A great theologian once pointed out to those who had difficulty entering an event long past that in God, everything is *now*, so when you are watching Jesus carry his cross, God the Father is simultaneously embracing Jesus carrying and you watching. This is mysterious business, but people's experiences are intense and undeniable. For instance, a scholarly man who had struggled with what he felt Scripture scholarship allowed him to accept in the stories of the Bible was definitively relieved of his mental blockage when he suddenly accepted the invitation to touch the wood of the cross.

In the evening during a retreat, after praying long hours in one of the events in Jesus' life, you might turn to a modification of this Ignatian contemplation. It is called "application of the senses," because you "taste and see" (Psalm 34:8) what you and Jesus have been through during the previous hours. This is a quiet, restful kind of prayer. You might well spend a whole hour with Jesus, just leaning against the stone wall around a garden, filled with a deep sense of communion but saying practically nothing.

At the end of every kind of Ignatian contemplation, you return to yourself as you are at the moment. Coming back into real time, you ask what the things you have felt and thought have to do with your own concerns. You "apply it to yourself," as Master Ignatius put it. And then you turn to the Father, or to Jesus of Nazareth, or even to a holy person who was part of the event to say what you want to say and ask what you want to ask. By then, you are surer that what you want and what God wants coincide.

Builders of the Kingdom

When you make the full Spiritual Exercises, you meditate several times on materials that Master Ignatius himself created. He found these materials helpful, and experience proved that others found them helpful as well. He was doing what Jesus had done: Jesus found considering the lilies of the field helpful and recommended the experience to others. Among the most characteristic of Ignatius's materials is a consideration of a great leader called "The Call of the King," which is a preparation for encountering Jesus' life.

The prayer begins with a fantasy about a great charismatic leader beset by enemies. The leader proposes a grand scheme to overcome all his enemies and establish a just reign. He warns his disciples that they will have to endure hard labor and suffering, and a great deal of both, but he promises that he will be there with them in all that they do and go through. And he promises with great authority that, in the end, he will overcome. A fantasy like this is easy for most of us to indulge, because such kings and princes populate the fables and novels of every people, and most human beings yearn to follow one.

In Ignatius's meditation, you ask yourself before the Lord, Who would not enlist in such a project with such a leader? Accepting the obvious answer, you turn to consider the One whom you wish to take as your leader. You let Jesus Christ speak about his grand scheme. Standing before the whole world, he announces the Father's will: a kingdom of justice and love in which all are equally welcome. He must lead his people, who are besieged by enemies. He knows—who better?—the cost of establishing this reign. But with divine authority, he will establish it.

Jesus of Nazareth gathered helpers to go into the world and spread the kingdom, the first intentionally global institution. Now the Holy Spirit does. Jesus' invitation "Follow me" is given in some manner to every Christian. Each of us baptized in Christ is called not only to live in the reign of God but also to help establish it. The call differs from person to person, because now, as in Jesus' lifetime, each person's unique call grows from and suits his or her concrete gifts, given by God our Creator and Lord.

All disciples are called to follow Christ in establishing the reign of God. All are called to live a life characterized by the Beatitudes, which are not moral mandates or promises of the future but a clear description of the way things are in the reign already established. The poor really are blessed; the meek actually are inheriting the earth. When we mourn, we are strengthened by the divine Comforter with the gift of hope.

Through the centuries, millions of men and women have lived this way. No one noted their holiness. They have not been canonized by a pope or even remembered by history. Yet they lived faithful to Jesus Christ, the King who called them, in the church. They confessed him in the creed and took him into themselves in communion. Many millions still live this way in the reign already established; by God's decree, this is the way they answer the call of the King.

Some of us, though, are called to go along with Jesus Christ in another way. The Holy Spirit and our own spirits (when we pray long and devoutly on the life of Jesus of Nazareth) bring us to ask Jesus Christ something out of the ordinary, something our life world will never comprehend. Master Ignatius wrote it into his text as a prayer, suggesting that we might want to say: "I protest that it is my earnest desire and my deliberate choice, provided only it is for Thy great service and praise, to imitate Thee in bearing all wrongs and all abuse and all poverty, both actual and spiritual, should Thy most holy majesty deign to choose and admit me to such a state and way of life."

There are those who say this prayer with a full heart. It is a mistake to imagine that they must surely shine among those who follow Christ the King. They rarely do. As did their Master at the Jordan, each seems to be just one more of the shaggy, marginalized crowd.

26

"As I Have Loved You"

Jesus of Nazareth instructed his disciples that they were to love one another the way he loved them. It might be helpful to consider how he loved, particularly since Ignatian spirituality thrives in the friendships of everyday life.

Early in Jesus' time around the Jordan, two disciples of John approached Jesus and asked where he was staying. Jesus invited them to "come and see" (John 1:39). The invitation is commonly considered a call to be apostles. But before it was a vocation, it was an invitation to friendship, given by the One who became their faithful friend.

Jesus got his earliest lessons in how to love in the secrecy of the hidden life in Nazareth, about which we know almost nothing. One thing we do know with certainty is that Jesus of Nazareth accepted the men and women whom the Father put into his life. He learned to be easy with fishermen, lawyers, and prostitutes. He liked little Zacchaeus and chose another tax collector, Levi, as an intimate. He used to talk through the night with Nicodemus, whom he knew well; he felt love on first sight for a rich young man. After the excitement of his entry into Jerusalem, he spent the night with his friends in Bethany (Matthew 21:17).

Like Bethany, places like Cana and Emmaus are associated with his gift for friendship. The more socially righteous considered him "a glutton and a drunkard, a friend of tax collectors and sinners" (Matthew 11:19), which Jesus seems not to have minded.

This making of friends was not a utilitarian tactic but the expression of the fullness of Jesus' humanity. Jesus is made, as we are, in the image and likeness of God, who is not only One but also Three. So to be a person is to be related. Jesus had to have friends, or he would have been incomplete in his humanity.

We know some things about the friendships of his maturity. The incident at the Jordan, for instance, suggests that friends are not so much found as made: they "stayed with him the rest of that day" (John 1:39). Other incidents show that Jesus chose his friends, praying beforehand: first there were seventy-two; then there were twelve; and gradually, there were the special three—Peter, James, and John. And there was "the disciple whom Jesus loved." All along—and quite contrary to his culture—Jesus had women friends by his side, including when he went around teaching.

What did he do with his friends? We know a lot, if we think about it. He showed them how to pray and prayed with them. He showed them how to go into silence and solitude. He led them to share his own ideal of a kingdom of love—he wanted them to be a community of love. He taught them to be poor in spirit, trusting the Father absolutely, but to keep a purse for the poor.

Perhaps most instructive of all, Jesus shared with his friends his own deepest concerns. He told them of his temptations in the desert. He brought the three to be with him when he was wrapped in ecstasy on the mountain and when he sweated in agony in the garden. He corrected them. He asked them what people thought of him. He depended on them; when others walked away, he worried that they, too, would go. And when they came back from good work, Jesus took them aside, "where they could be by themselves" (Luke 9:10) and share experiences.

More than one spiritual guide has remarked that those who do not have good friends do not get very far into friendship with Jesus of Nazareth. The operative truth may be that they do not know how to be friends. Jesus did; he created and lived in a communion of persons, sharing purse, work, talk, rest. Coming to know him, we all come to know our self better, that self made in the image of the Firstborn.

27

The Language of the Cross

Some suggestions given by Master Ignatius for praying on Jesus' passion help bring it into the ordinary days of our life. We begin, as in any other contemplation, by asking who is present, what they are saying, and what they are doing. But we go on to do three things: We consider what Jesus suffered in his humanity and "what he wanted to suffer." We consider how the divinity hid himself, not intervening. And then we beg to appreciate that Jesus did this for us.

Jesus' brutal physical sufferings can be painted and sculpted, but it is not so easy to put the human part of what he suffered into words. Perhaps we have to start with this: Jesus was the victim of political and religious abuses. His murder was politically inane, because in the long run the abuse of political power with violence wipes out what it pretends to achieve: right order. Then again, his execution was religiously senseless, because right from the start violent religious persecution destroys the holiness of the persecutor, and holiness is what religion is about. So Jesus suffered an inane and senseless horror, an experience only too many of us are familiar with today. This is what he "wanted to suffer": to live to the very end in solidarity with humankind, familiar with inanity and meaninglessness.

Jesus suffered as we all suffer. Each one of us, when we suffer bitterly, can hardly believe that there exists any suffering like our own. But suffering is like language: my words are not merely mine; however much I have made them my own, they belong to all of us. Suffering is among us, and no suffering is any one person's possession. I can talk about "my" cancer, but many others around me are suffering with it, too.

None of us is at all likely to suffer the physical torture that Jesus suffered (God grant this freedom to us all). But each one of us inescapably suffers physical pains and decay. This human suffering that afflicts all of us is what Jesus *wanted* to suffer. He was no masochist. He chose to embrace even bitter suffering so that he could be like us in everything—except sin—and by his obedience turn the whole of human experience from its journey into death and onto the way of eternal life.

Master Ignatius tells the one praying on Jesus' passion to "begin with great effort to strive to grieve, be sad, and weep." It is never easy to suffer, and it is particularly difficult to enter into another's suffering. We have to work to grasp that Jesus, on his cross, knew the terrifying vacuum of God's hiding and leaving him to the merciless experiences that scotch life. Most of us will sink into that dreadful feeling at some point in the chaos of our world.

Despair is a choice just as much as hope is a choice, and Jesus did not suffer despair because he refused to. He trusted that the Father would save him; he said more than once that he would die and that he expected to rise from the dead. On the cross, he trusted that his suffering made some kind of sense, to be revealed when the Father chose. Every day of his human life, he wanted to do whatever he could to alleviate the suffering of those around him. But he was thwarted. He had to die in the hope that he would live again in our flesh.

Those who really do know and love him will suffer this way, his way. They will also see the suffering of all the people whom God puts in their life world and strive with great effort to grieve with them and do whatever they can to alleviate their suffering. Right here is the deepest spiritual root of the impulse to work for peace and justice. Anything less would be an unworthy motive for those who love Jesus Christ.

Jesus' passion brings us to embrace the world as it really is: full of violence and pain. We refuse to let religion and grace become an easy analgesic, buffering us from the real sufferings around us. Instead, we embrace whatever suffering comes into our lives as no longer senseless. Our suffering has a meaning in "the language of the cross" (1 Corinthians 1:18). We join the sufferings of the crucified Christ, the sufferings of humankind that he chose to embrace. We cling to Jesus, to "a Christ who is the power and the wisdom of God" (1 Corinthians 1:24). When we do less, we are using our faith in Christ as a pain pill.

28

The Joy of the Consoler

W hat Jesus meant when he said, "My joy I give you" begins to make sense when we contemplate his resurrection (see John 17:13). What was Jesus' experience of coming back alive into our flesh? Part of it we can never fathom: Jesus of Nazareth is now the Christ, "the first-fruits of all who have fallen asleep" (1 Corinthians 15:20). The almighty Father has brought everything together under Christ as head, "everything in the heavens and everything on earth" (Colossians 1:20). This mystery will be revealed with all its glory at the end-time.

We can, however, enter into the joy of the Jesus who delighted in the children of the world. We are among the Lord's creation now and will rise among it again, when our time comes. Meanwhile, we can ask to live joyfully, as Jesus lived. In fact, we will not serve God well except in joy; of the gifts that the Holy Spirit pours out on the elect, Paul lists joy right after love, the first (Galatians 5:22).

What did Jesus feel when he came alive again in the flesh? His first joy was simply to be alive again, something we might experience after a life-threatening unconsciousness or a brush with death. Jesus appreciated his humanity, the gift of the Father.

He loved the lilies of the field and the birds of the air and the people around him.

When Jesus rose, he went first of all to his mother. Even though this is not recorded in the Gospels, anyone with sense knows he did it, as Master Ignatius remarked in *The Spiritual Exercises*. That meeting might well have been the most intensely joyous human encounter ever. Then Jesus went to others whom he loved. It was a joy simply to show himself to them and let them know that he lived again. This is a joy that we can enter into if we are willing to open ourselves to those whom God gives us. Jesus enjoyed saying to a grief-stricken woman, "Mary!" Then Magdalene held him to her heart until he sent her to tell the news to the rest. (This is how he will treat anyone who comes to love him.)

When he went to his own, Jesus took great joy in showing that he forgave those who had abandoned him. He did not, as far as we know, tell them that he forgave them. He just did the forgiving. That may be why he went to Peter first. Later, he drew the poison out of Peter's self-doubt by seeming to share it. As if to reassure himself, he asked Peter three times whether he loved him. He already knew, of course; it was Peter he wanted to reassure. By showing his forgiveness, Jesus made Peter's love as unshakable as a rock. We all know the joy of making someone love us whom we already love.

Jesus' joy came also with repairing the disciples' hope for the kingdom, a hope that his rejection and death had deadened. They were not hopeful when they locked themselves into the upper room. He brought them hope by suddenly standing in the midst of them. The risen Christ also made sure that his friends then and now understand that we are not going anywhere. We will live forever in the flesh that we now know, though taken up into incorruptibility. To assure them of this, Jesus ate with them—in the upper room, on the seashore, in Emmaus. And he touched and asked to be touched: "Give me your hand," he said to Thomas (John 20:27). And then they all believed.

The risen Christ's ministry is one of reconciliation. This ministry is an important component in the Ignatian way of living. Every culture, in its various ways, is marred by disordered and broken relationships. Family members are alienated from one another. Siblings and friends live in constant conflict, or resolutely refuse intimacy and hold one another at arm's length. Individuals live too dependent on one another and even enable one another's addictions. We are—every single one of us—wounded.

Why did Jesus keep in his body the vivid wounds that brought about his death? He came back to console his disciples and to send them to console others, and he did so by showing them that he was wounded, as they were wounded.

Even though they were wounded, he sent them. But before he did, he asked for something to eat in order to allay their stupefaction. There is something rich about Jesus holding a piece of bread or fish in a pierced hand. He did nothing meaningless, so it calls for explanation. He must have been smiling.

29

Spiritual Consolation

Ignatian spirituality gives careful attention to what it calls "consolation." The gifts given by the Holy Spirit to the baptized—love, joy, peace, patience, kindness, goodness, trustfulness, gentleness, and self-control—surely add up to consolation, as every great spiritual tradition recognizes.

In Ignatian spirituality, the term has a rather more distinct meaning. Living in consolation means that you effectively put God first and readily bypass anything that might cut you off from God. There will be feeling involved in this, of course, but the unique sign that you love God above all rises in what you do. An Ignatian summary of spiritual consolation is that you "love God in all things and all things in God." You trust God easily, almost automatically. You feel hopeful about your life and affairs, and even while you are fully aware of the violent evils raking the globe, you believe that the almighty Creator and Lord still governs human affairs, and all will be well in the end.

Spiritual consolation is the soul weather that makes it easy for you to do good, in the way a sunny day makes it easy for flowers to bloom. Let's say, for instance, that a close friend dies a tragic death when you are young. You are deeply grieved, and yet you say with your whole heart that your friend is better off than we are. When you are more mature, you are tempted to abandon some good action you had decided to do but feel the strength to go through with it. These are times of consolation.

You may feel good when you are in consolation, tranquil or perhaps even exultant. We expect to feel good in life and have a right to. But the feelings are not the core of consolation. For there are times when you may feel emotionally dejected, but if you keep trusting God and hoping with determination, and if you will not give up loving God, then you are in consolation. Your soul may feel empty when, at great cost, you achieve reconciliation with an enemy. You are nonetheless in consolation if you love God steadily and wish good for the offender.

This interplay between feeling and fact might seem a little clearer in light of the difference between happiness and joy. The world can give happiness, along with riches and power and friendship—and the world can take it away. The Spirit gives joy, along with trust and love—and nothing the world can do could take it away. Only the Holy Spirit can take it away, though you yourself can squander this gift like any other.

Ordinarily, consolation comes to us as we live out the life that the Spirit calls us to live. Those who are called to live an intense interior life will know keen sweetness in loving Jesus Christ and may be given powerful insights and enlightenment. But most of the time, and for most of us, consolation comes in a more pedestrian shape. You feel deep joy when worshipping God on Sundays or simply saying your favorite prayers. You go to daily prayer without fuss and think and pray with few disturbances. Away from prayer, at work, you quietly do what you must do, serenely and honestly. Not a lot causes you any great upset.

Consolation tells us that we are living the way the Spirit calls us to live. We simply know that we are who God hopes we will be and that we are doing what God hopes we will do. We find it easy to give thanks.

During most of our waking lives, we do and avoid things to sustain the consolation that the Spirit gives us. But sometimes, consolation comes to us directly from the Holy Spirit, without any forewarning and without any particular connection to anything we are doing or thinking. We suddenly know, deep in the marrow of our bones, that God lives and cherishes us. Or perhaps we solve a conundrum of long standing, its solution given to us whole. Or we discover that we have already embraced a bitterly difficult task and are no longer afraid.

Ignatian spirituality calls this "consolation without previous cause." The Spirit has chosen to come into our life—as is the Spirit's privilege. Our work here is to say yes and to get on with what God gives us to do.

30

Spiritual Desolation

It happens to all of us: an ugly revelation makes us lose hope in the church, or a personal failure makes us deeply disgusted with life, and we sadly pull back into ourselves. We stop sharing with those we love; we keep secrets from our spiritual friends. We feel that we are not doing any good in life. Sometimes we feel abandoned and are just not sure that God cares about us—or that God really orders all things from end to end.

When this happens, we have moved from the way we are meant to live, in consolation, and into spiritual desolation. What is desolation? It means weaker faith, dimmer hope, and faltering love. You start trusting your insurance policies instead of God. What does God care? You despair of your chosen way of life having any meaning. You are not even sure you love yourself (violating the last phrase of the great commandment), and when you try to pray, all you feel is emptiness.

Desolation is not quite the same as psychological depression or dejection, though these moods commonly come along with it. We can be dejected about the violence in the world without losing hope that our God reigns. We can be seriously depressed that our children are leaving the church without feeling that God has somehow let us down.

Nor is desolation a terminal spiritual illness, because Jesus Christ has overcome not only death and sin but also their daily concomitants, the bane of desolation among them. Further, we know that desolation and consolation come and go, like winter and summer on earth, even in the lives of those who love God faithfully. You need to remember why they do: the spirit of evil still stalks the earth as it did in Jesus' time. Spiritual desolation brings into your self the life-and-death struggle between good and evil that God has allowed to continue. Evil gave Jesus some bad moments; why not you?

The spirit of evil brings desolation of itself; it spreads lies and works through deceit. The disciple of Christ experiences desolation wherever these things are. Evil visits the earth in violence, and desolation usually brings vehement feelings and harsh judgments. Embrace such spirits and you are betraying the Spirit that Jesus Christ and the Father sent upon the earth.

Evil wants one of two things. Either it wants you to quit doing the good that you are doing, or it wants you to be desolate even though you are living a good life. For example, you are working well with friends when one of them insults you. The evil spirit will urge revenge, and if you take it, you will not work well with friends, and you have stopped doing the good you were doing. Embracing the desire for revenge was itself a desolation. Sin thrives in the climate of desolation the way mold grows when the weather is damp.

But suppose that you brush away that temptation. Do not think that the evil spirit quits. For if evil cannot lure you away from doing good, it will still try to make you less joyful doing it. You will find yourself less content to be working with your friends. You will feel distrustful of them and justify the feeling to yourself. If evil cannot make you fail Jesus Christ by losing faith and hope and pulling away from love, then it will try to keep you from enjoying the life Christ calls you to.

People who do not know Christ do the best they can to find happiness. Even when they glitter and exude power, they live desolate lives. Why the frenzy of fashion and drugs and entertainment? You are called to a different way.

.... **31** ....

The Meaning of Desolation

Spiritual desolation weighs heavy on us, so it is useful to recall how we get into it. First of all, we put ourselves in desolation by choosing to live against our consciences or against the authentic teachings of the church. If you choose to despise the people in your parish, you are not going to feel joy at communion. The man who never shares his food with the hungry will find no joy in it (though he may well get fat happily).

When you are going from sin to sin without paying much attention, the Holy Spirit can hardly continue to lavish gifts on you. You are wasting the gifts already given. So the Spirit will let you feel the weight of your sin: the loss of faith and hope and love. The evil spirit, of course, would like you to go right on sinning. A married woman with a career was neglecting her family seriously but "felt good about it" because she was getting ahead. As Jesus said, "If you belonged to the world, the world would love you as its own" (John 15:19). Her world loved her as its own. She tried to pray daily but felt desolate and quit before long.

What about people who go from good to good? Even those of us who go to Mass regularly and pray daily find ourselves desolate at times. Why? Master Ignatius identified three situations. The first is when we grow negligent in our practice of religion and lazy in our interior lives. When you start wondering what you "get out of Mass," you are on the way to desolation. A good man once wondered why he was feeling dejected and gave himself the answer when he admitted that he was not praying as he had committed himself to. Of course, when we neglect God we grow desolate. God is love, and love does not willingly abide neglect for long.

In the second situation, we find ourselves desolate even though we judge that we are doing everything we are supposed to do. A likely cause is the subtle belief that we have been earning consolation. We can earn happiness, along with a lot of money and social position. We cannot earn the gifts of the Spirit, and God cannot let us think that we do. Consolation is Christ's gift, given "so that my own joy may be in you and your joy be complete" (John 15:11). Sometimes we think we deserve God's gifts; the Holy Spirit will not console us for this error.

The third situation arises in the lives of those who are serious in serving God and others. Sometimes God simply wants to let you feel the strength of your faith and hope and love, to know the power and depth of his gifts, so he takes away the good feelings and the sweetness, the deeply human pleasures that mark his gifts of grace, while leaving you with trust and love. When that happens, you can do no more than hold on to the One whom you love and keep on doing the next good thing. In time, the Spirit will come again with consolation—often enough, greater than you have known before.

Far from passively accepting desolation, we need to resist it. How? By going against the temptation to just quit or slack off. In desolation, we ordinarily do well to increase our prayer and good acts. That may seem obvious, but it is not easy for the simple reason that in desolation, we feel distaste for anything spiritual at all, and the mildest prayer pesters us like a green persimmon pesters our mouth. Unless we resist, we are likely to turn to sensual pseudo-consolations, to eating and drinking and sexual irresponsibility.

Notice that while we cannot earn our consolations, we do usually earn our desolations, bringing them on ourselves by our sins and negligence. When we are desolate, then, we need to be patient with ourselves and with God, resolutely accepting whatever the Spirit of Jesus Christ puts into our spirit here and now, leaving the rest, the past and the future, where it belongs—in God.

Ignatian Discernment of Spirits

Human beings are moved by a dense complex of motives, both in the things we do from day to day and in our big decisions. What drives a young woman to become a doctor or a young man to be an engineer? Many things contribute: success, altruism, interest. Or what drives a woman who has smoked for years to quit or an obese man to get thin? Again, many things contribute: fear of death, desire for health, concern of family. But they all interact in a kind of movement that eventually drives the person to act. Master Ignatius learned to think about those dense complexes of motives—images, ideas, attractions, revulsions—as "spirits."

We can all name many spirits. There is school spirit, in which everyone cheers together for the football team. There is fear, which can depress an entire city, and exultation, which can cause a whole nation to rise up. But spirits are not only secular. A thrill of devotion fills St. Peter's Square when a saint is canonized. A spirit of prayer drives people to make retreats. Christians under atheistic despotisms are moved to remain faithful.

Master Ignatius noted that these dense complexes of motives and energies take on two configurations, which he identified with consolation and desolation. He discovered that both consolation and desolation can move you toward God or pull you away from God. Then he noted that sometimes consolation comes from a good spirit and sometimes from a bad spirit, and he noted the same thing about desolation.

Ignatian spirituality applies this to interpreting major decisions and daily experience as well. The movement of spirits, obviously, involves a set of complex variables: consolation and desolation, good and evil spirits, movements to and away from God. Not everyone can master Ignatian discernment of spirits, and not everyone will want to try. Ignatian guides set great store by it, though, and a lot of people get the gist of it and apply it. A recent book described how a parent used discernment to help her teenager daughter decide how far she wanted to conform her behavior to current fads.

Some basic patterns are easy to grasp. For instance, as you would anticipate, the good spirit usually brings love, joy, peace, and the like; the evil spirit characteristically brings confusion, doubt, disgust, and the like. Another pattern: when you are leading a seriously sinful life, a good spirit will visit you with desolation to turn you around; an evil spirit will keep you content so that you will keep sinning. Another clear pattern is the opposite of this: when you are seriously serving God, the spirits change roles. The evil spirit clouds your day with desolation to lead you away from God, while the good spirit fills your day with trust and love of God. And a final, easily grasped pattern: a spirit that works in light and openness is good, while a spirit cloaked in secrecy and deception is evil.

Some basic practices are also easy to figure out. When you have made a good decision to serve God better and after awhile go into desolation, you should not change the decision; it's hardly a good spirit moving you. When you are feeling down, you would do well to pray a little more and increase the help you give to others. When, without warning or any preparatory activity, you are consoled with the love of God above all things, you can trust that it is a good spirit (particularly if it comes with tears). But when you are thinking or praying and grow consoled or disconsolate—well, test those movements. They could come from either spirit, as we have seen.

There is a good deal more to Ignatian discernment, and it gets no simpler. It is not, however, a merely human discipline. "Now instead of the spirit of the world, we have received the Spirit that comes from God, to teach us to understand the gifts that he has given us" (1 Corinthians 2:12). Serious disciples cherish this gift and put it to good use.

Humility and Greatness

True humility does not attract many in this new age of self-realization. We tend to equate humility with self-abasement, but such "humility" would attract only the mentally ill, and it is not Christian humility.

If you cling to a negative self-image and have no great respect for your gifts, you are not being humble. You are showing no gratitude to God, who gave you the gifts, and this sin of ingratitude provides the deepest wellspring of every other sin. You hate yourself, whom God loves. This fake humility masks a flinty pride: you refuse to love the gifts and even the self that God is giving you. This is a self-deceiving way of telling God, "I will not serve."

Christian humility, properly understood, requires a strong sense of self, and the greater the humility, the stronger the sense of self. For as more than one saint has remarked, humility is seeing and acknowledging the truth about yourself and your world. If you are smart, you are lying—not being humble—if you act as though you are not. Consider this: Jesus Christ, the Son of God, said that he was "gentle and humble in heart" (Matthew 11:29), and all four Gospels tell of a man who knew perfectly well who he was, a man with an unshakably strong sense of self.

All spiritualities describe humility and, since spirituality guides life, explain how it is lived. Ignatian spirituality describes humility in terms of loving Jesus Christ and notes that it can be lived in three ways. Each way leads you to Jesus Christ and to live progressively more as he lived. God our Creator and Lord calls each person to one of these ways—though you are always free to beg the Lord to move you along in love.

The first way is fundamental. You love Jesus Christ so much that nothing and no one on earth could persuade you to do what you know would cut you off from him. The celebrant at Mass begs Jesus Christ just before communion, "Never let me be separated from you." Doing what the love of Christ requires, you become a lover, for love is what you do, not merely how you feel or what you proclaim. So you are a lover, perhaps not a very passionate one, but at the least one who says, "I would never do what you don't want." If you live that way in the church, you live like a good citizen who loves his country and keeps its laws but does not vote or take much interest in its affairs. When you follow this first way of humility, you will certainly have to act courageously in your life world.

Or you can be another kind of lover and live humbly in a second way. You love Jesus Christ so much that you want to remain loyal even to his great redemptive vision. You want to understand what Christ hopes for in the world and particularly in the church. You find real meaning in the Beatitudes. You refuse to hate your nation's enemies and you forgive those who hurt you, as he forgave even those who nailed him to the cross. You reject the infidelities in the church but not the faithful men and women whom God has chosen—none of whom are any better than you.

To those of us who live humility in this second way, Jesus is important in the way that great, charismatic leaders are important. We follow great leaders passionately but at a distance, because their greatness and their charisms stand between us and them. We love them as people loved Napoléon or Winston Churchill: as a persona rather than an intimately known person.

If you follow Jesus in this second way, you are the kind of lover who says, "I want to do whatever you want." Make no mistake about it: doing all of what Jesus wants demands a strong sense of self. You are proclaiming a desire to be a close follower of Jesus Christ, who asks us all to take up our cross daily.

The Third Degree of Humility

The third way to live humility in Ignatian spirituality begins with a prayer to the Father that he will grant you the grace to live in the way of Jesus, who "emptied himself to assume the condition of a slave" (Philippians 2:7). It leads to choosing things that your life world despises.

Here's an illustration: A man is at the peak of his career. He is doing great good in his work, has grown quite wealthy, and his whole city knows how good he is. Then he meets Jesus Christ in prayer and hears the call of the King. That call is to leave his success and wealth behind and help the men and women who are hungry and homeless in his community. So he does that, simply because he loves his Master and wants to be like him. The man resigns his position and begins to manage soup kitchens.

This lover asks the Father, "Let me do things together with your Son and like your Son." He is opening himself to some negative things and some positive things. He is saying to God that he will set aside anything in his life or his self that stands between him and the One he loves. He will not cling to any attitude or habit that would make him other than who Jesus of Nazareth was and is.

But there is more. He understands that God may have hopes for him that require his setting aside some strong and great gifts. The man in the illustration had a great talent for business, and he let it go. He had great potential as a civic leader, and he abandoned that potential. More than one superbly gifted musician has laid instrument and music aside because God called him or her to something different.

Is this moral? Is this not despising the gifts of God? It could be. But that is not likely if the lover has a strong sense of self, knows his or her gifts, and appreciates them for what they really are. But there is something that the lover appreciates more: doing everything together with Jesus Christ. The Beloved has lived a certain kind of life, so this lover wants to live it, too.

Is this real? It is, and we have seen many instances of it. Many of Christ's disciples today live among the poor and outcast because of love for Jesus Christ. Many others set aside the deep human instinct to propagate because they are called as Jesus was to generate life in another way. Others, both married and single, empty themselves to serve as the Master did and let no one know what it costs except the One whom they love.

This third degree of humility often brings to mind images of someone despised and rejected, as Jesus was in the end. It may be that God the Father would choose that for the one who asks to live as the Son lived. It certainly happens: those who proclaim the Good News are incarcerated for long years, for instance. But it is crucial to note that if someone provokes others to despise and reject him except when he is doing what must be done for Christ's sake, he cannot be thought humble. A fool, perhaps; not humble. Always the prayer must be that the Father allow you to imitate in your own time the way of Jesus of Nazareth, so long as you do not sin, and no one else sins, either.

The lover in this case is made greater by love. The Beloved chose to empty himself, taking on the ways and characteristics of a servant. He did not mind being told that he was seriously mistaken about God and the people. He did not mind being considered mad. And his way led to great suffering and death. The person who wishes to be meek and humble as Jesus was can say to the Father honestly, "Treat me as you treated your own Son." Such a prayer has nothing to do with negative self-image or despising the gifts of the Spirit. On the contrary, heroic love is meek and humble, but it is also glorifying. Just look at what happened in the end to Jesus of Nazareth.

35

Making Choices

No matter how stable a lifestyle our personal vocation may call for, today's world makes change unavoidable. Even men and women who chose stability in a monastery have had to manage steady change. Most of the change we encounter requires making choices. Sometimes these choices are between good and evil. More often for those of us who are intent on serving God, they are between two good things or even among many good things. For example, a mother can take a job in order to raise her family's style of life or remain home and raise the level of care for her children.

All of this means that even after we have obeyed our conscience, we still face choices of consequence throughout our lives. How are we going to make them?

When we are making a decision more serious than whether to take a cup of tea, we will first of all intend to serve God. Then we will decide what else we intend. How will we set our hearts "on his kingdom first, and on his righteousness" (Matthew 6:33)? This is not such a simple matter. Some faithful disciples work to get rich, simply expecting (when they think about it) that they will serve God as rich people. That looks a lot like putting money before God. Still, there is nothing wrong with getting rich—provided we are getting rich by trying to do what God wants.

We come to know what God wants in many ways. God has revealed some of what he wants to even the simplest among us by giving us the commandments and the disciplines of the church. Many of Jesus' disciples live good lives by following these.

Others among us are drawn to go deeper into what God wants. We choose to live an interior life, and we make no choices of any importance without prayer. In Ignatian spirituality, we also depend on the movements in us that the Holy Spirit stirs. Consolation suggests that we have made a good choice; desolation suggests that we should step back and take another look. Sometimes the Spirit moves us to go ahead; other times, to wait upon the Lord.

It is worth noting a couple of distinctions that apply to any choice among many good options. First, you can make good decisions and bad decisions. A good decision grows out of your gifts and your graced history in Christ; it is one that Jesus Christ calls you to. A bad decision goes against your gifts or history and moves you away from God, even if by the tiniest step.

Second, you can make good decisions well or badly. A decision made with a wise understanding of the way things are, and not out of ignorance or daydreams, is well made. A decision made with prayer and, often, with the companionship of a spiritual friend is well made. And those who know themselves make decisions well. A decision made badly just happens without any clear choice, or takes shape in some sinful desire or unreflected-upon conviction that has moved you.

Making good decisions is doing what God wants done; making bad decisions is attempting to drag God our Creator and Lord along with our own plans for the universe. Just as we can make a good decision badly, such as planning to go to Sunday Mass if the sun is out and going when it is, we can also, more subtly, make a bad decision well, such as choosing after some prayer and advice to remain a celibate, only to discover through moral failures that celibacy is not where the Spirit calls.

The Spirit of Christ can call for a revision of any decision, which reminds us of a truly fundamental truth: When we decide that we have discerned what God wants done and choose to do it, we have not reached certainty. We have reached hope-filled enactment.

A sound spirituality accounts for all of the complex variables at work in making good decisions well. They all twine around the core issue in any serious choice among good things: what is it we most authentically desire? Ignatian spirituality takes as axiomatic that because we are sinful, we do not easily discover what we most authentically desire. This has two consequences. The first is that those who are called to a spiritual life are going to have to pray daily. Not doing so means growing deaf to that call. And the second is that spiritual companionship is not a luxury, but a necessity. From everything we know about Jesus of Nazareth, he needed it.

36

The Two Standards

J esus contrasted his way to the way of the world quite emphatically: "He who is not with me is against me" (Luke 11:23). Master Ignatius helps us apply this to ourselves in a key meditation in the Spiritual Exercises called "A Meditation on the Two Standards"—a "standard" meaning a flag.

Some people who make the full Exercises choose to make an offering "of greater moment" (in Master Ignatius's phrase), asking the Father to allow them to live as Jesus lived, committing their whole self and life to God. Many in the postconciliar church—married as well as single, lay as well as clerical—are given that grace. Women have left everything behind and gone to help in underdeveloped countries, for instance, and men still risk everything to embrace the celibate priesthood.

The choice between the two standards, however, is not restricted to those who make an offering of greater moment. All disciples have to choose where we are going to stand—with Jesus or with the world. No matter what life the Spirit has drawn us to, once we are baptized and confirmed we are called to stand in Jesus' company under his flag.

We begin to move under Jesus' standard when we join him in the living conviction that everything we have and are is God's gift. However much or little we have, we say gratefully, "Look at all God has given me." Then the way opens through the smoke of self-satisfaction and approval of others. "How can I help?" becomes a daily preoccupation. And through a life of love and service, the Spirit leads us to live as meekly and humbly as the Lord lived—whether we are a famous ballerina or an anonymous computer programmer.

The way of the world differs entirely. The starting point is getting as much wealth as you can. You say, "Look at all this stuff I have." When the world's way opens before you, you shift your focus, saying, "Look at me with all this stuff." As those around you grow more deferential, you start saying, "Look at *me*." You become convinced that you are the center of your world. You may not have sinned yet, but it is only a matter of time.

Even without subscribing to theories of the subconscious, we can see that the world's standard is as inviting to Christ's disciples as it is to anyone else. In a way, even after we have made a solemn, lifelong choice to follow Christ's standard, we have to purify our daily life of collusion with the world's standard. The collusion comes in three forms.

First, there is benign secularism. Certainly, there are people who do not know Jesus Christ who lead deeply good lives. But even the baptized can live in a benignly secular way. We join civic movements and help the needy because that's what our neighbors do. We are good to our families and honest in the workplace. There is no immediate harm in this way, but neither is there anything more than a secular spirit, even though people today call it spirituality.

The second form of collusion, seen particularly in the affluent first world, is the search for pleasure. We are surrounded by people who live what St. Paul describes as the way of the flesh.

Those who follow this way are the target of advertising; they need to have whatever everyone else has right now. Their less lovely side manifests self-indulgence, lust, envy—all seen as acceptable social mores. The flesh has its own laws, and those who follow this way will readily obey those laws into sin.

Finally, there is the collusion of succumbing to darkness. Think of the report of an adult who forced a twelve-year-old to kill another and then drink some of his blood. It is evil manifest. But most of the works of the dark are not manifest. Hatred, vengeance, violence, self-destructive habits—these flourish in the dark corners of the sinful human self.

In your heart of hearts, you may loathe the dark and leap to the light. But in everyday life, you will find yourself in the twilight of benign secularism or the flesh over and over again. You will find safety in Christ's standard only if you resolutely begin everything with thanks to God and keep watching what you are doing and why you are doing it.

37

Food for the Hungry

A ll spiritualities and all religions lay down standards about eating and drinking. Devout Muslims keep a strenuous fast for a month each year, and orthodox Jews eat only kosher foods. The Catholic Church, in living memory, assigned numerous days for fasting and abstaining from meat. But the post-conciliar church has not yet reorganized standards on food and drink. This seems like a weakness; it certainly throws us on our own resources.

Food and drink are among God's most abundant gifts, glorious creations meant to help us know and love God and one another. Perhaps we have not been availing ourselves of them very wisely. Much of the world's population is badly nourished: one-third because the people eat too little, sadly having no more, and one-third because the people have nothing and are starving. Yet in our affluent part of the world, obesity is a grave problem even among children. We may be keenly aware of this in theory and perhaps worry about Jesus' account of the Last Judgment (Matthew 25:41–42, 46). But no one who is mindful of others' hunger eats mindlessly whatever comes to hand.

Ignatian spirituality suggests an approach to food discipline that fits our current situation well. The starting point is simple: as with all of God's gifts, we must keep sensible order in our eating and drinking, serving God and not our taste buds. Obesity, unless it is an intractable medical disorder, is strong evidence of a spiritual disorder, an unruly appetite eroding spiritual and even moral freedom. Few disordered appetites seem to be as rampant in the world as the ones that feed obesity.

Ignatian norms for the diet share a number of points with every diet being promoted today: You take personal responsibility for your own nourishment. You decide what you are going to eat and how much. You put nourishment first and enjoyment second. Even more, you make your eating serve some higher needs than enjoyment: good nutrition, for instance, or a healthy heart.

Millions of people who are too well fed take up dieting, perhaps mainly out of vanity but also to improve nourishment. Suppose you decide that all motives for dieting are fine, but there is one better than any of them: that God our Lord gives food as a gift to all, and we are meant to use it in an orderly way so that we can share.

Here are some Ignatian guidelines for managing that: You are likely to eat in moderation those things that simply nourish, like bread or soup. You are likely to find it easier to abuse wine than water. Gourmet dishes you want to eat sparingly; really good cooking makes you want to eat a lot. You can more readily discover how much you should eat by beginning with real fasts (which, done moderately, have never hurt anyone) than by whittling down the calories. As in any diet, you decide well before every meal what you mean to have.

We can be helped greatly in using food and drink to the glory of God by remembering that Jesus enjoyed eating with friends. Judging by the stories that have come down to us, he enjoyed the friends more than the food. Imitate him. You can merely eat like the other animals, or you can dine with temperance and grace; do the latter, as Jesus did. The only time we hear about Jesus simply eating is after the Resurrection, when he asked for food so the disciples would know that he was not a ghost (ghosts do not eat honeycombs or fish). Otherwise, he was reclining at table, talking and listening. Dining is helped by good conversation or watching an interesting show on television.

Is this spirituality? It is on one condition: that you are doing it for God's sake and for the sake of your spiritual freedom. If you live in plenty, you are given plenty by God, who wishes you to use it for freedom. You eat to live; you do not live to eat. You want to find God in everything, and he has chosen in a stunning way to remain in food and drink—the Bread of Life and the cup of everlasting salvation. What a pity to abuse those gifts.

38

Scruples and Perfectionism

Ignatian spirituality has a way of dealing with scruples that may not seem very useful today. Who is scrupulous anymore? Who worries deeply that he has broken the fast required to receive communion? If a man came repeatedly for reconciliation with a fear like that, he would probably be advised to consult a psychiatrist. But this does not mean that the norms for handling scruples can be tossed into history's dustbin.

Some people who come for spiritual counsel today have interior lives that richly nourish the root from which the thornbush of scrupulosity used to grow. The root has not withered; it just pushes up a different thornbush. St. John Cassian and St. Thomas Aquinas called the root sloth, the capital sin. We think of it as merely laziness, but of course there are layers and layers beneath merely being lazy. Cassian and Aquinas judged that the ultimate reason why anyone would be lazy is that she does not accept the gifts that God pours on her. She feels worthless, not particularly good or useful.

The capital sins, as they are called, are configurations of the human personality that make an individual prone to one or another kind of sin. Envy unbalances a man's life in Christ the way asthma unbalances a man's physical life: it may not kill him, but it makes it difficult for him to breathe freely in Christ. Sloth makes us prone to any number of disorders, beginning with boredom (in prayer, work, life itself), which is the weight of unused abilities. The disorders born of sloth also include laziness, an absence of the sense of having an original purpose. Oddly, sloth gives rise to what the West calls workaholism: a man cannot not work; a woman can never be at leisure. As one workaholic said in anguish: "What am I trying to prove? And to whom?" He was trying to prove that he was worth anything at all, and to himself first of all. That is sloth.

Among those who lead a serious spiritual life, sloth manifests itself most commonly in perfectionism. It is the rare priest, for instance, who talks about his prayer without admitting at the start that he does not pray very well. How many of us go from one spiritual movement to another—from Cursillos de Cristiandad to Christian Life Community to the Exercises in daily life—always trying to get "holier"? Those of us who do this are the modern equivalent of Cassian's vagabond monk, the poor fellow who moved from one monastery to another, convinced that the next one would make him holy. The problem was in the monk, not in the monastery. And the problem in the monk was sloth, the sin of not accepting humbly the gifts that God is pouring in us right where we are standing—in the monastery or in our life world.

Perfectionism affects our interior lives first by making us feel that our gifts are not really adequate for us to love Christ (a feeling sometimes wrongly identified as humility). It also causes us to think and judge incorrectly. We think that we are somehow failing God and (mostly) ourselves, because, for instance, we do not go to daily Mass. Instead of gratefully accepting the gift of brief daily prayer, we aggravate ourselves with the thought that we should really be praying for a full hour.

When correctly interpreted, these thoughts and feelings can indeed lead us to greater holiness. Unhappily, the spirit of darkness takes hold of them and drives good people to desolation and then to relinquishing the good that they do. Worldwide, Christians complain about having a negative self-image and live as anxiously as anyone else. Our anxiety can be genuinely sinful, the fever of the sickness of perfectionism. Nothing we do is enough. We really should somehow be better than we are. We reach a point where we effectively demand more and better gifts from God, and, not getting them, we refuse to live joyful lives. This is a sin against the love of the One who gives us life.

The Ignatian solution for this resides in a trustworthy friend in the Lord who can be an authority figure in the sufferer's life. This might be a confessor, a spiritual guide, or simply a spiritual friend who can hold up the mirror of wisdom and tell us when we suffer that we can correctly and freely thank God for who and what we are.

Belonging in the Church

W hen we receive Holy Communion, we know in our hearts that we are receiving the Son of God. What we see is a wafer and a bit of wine. But our spirits, in union with the church, recognize him at the breaking of the bread.

Thinking with the church is so important a matter that Master Ignatius declared that if he thought something black and the church declared it white, he would see white. This may seem excessive to many today, when so much of Catholic belief and practice is contested. But just as much, if not more, was contested as Ignatian spirituality was taking shape during the Reformation. Then as now, all who wished to live consoled in a church *semper reformanda*, "always reforming," needed some sensible norms to follow. Master Ignatius supplied them in the last paragraphs of *The Spiritual Exercises*, and they can be applied to our experience today.

The norms rise from gratitude for the church, the Mystical Body of Christ. We begin by being thankful for the church reformed by the Second Vatican Council. We thank God for making the

Scriptures available to all, through both scholarship and methods of praying. We are thankful that we talk and listen lovingly to Christians separated from Rome; that we are free to explore the spiritual wealth of other religions, East and West; and that in each local church, we worship in our own language after centuries of mystification. We thank God that the council declared this time the age of the laity, insisting that each of us has a personal vocation and that the laity has its proper apostolic call in the marketplace.

Anyone who lives Ignatian spirituality chooses to be glad about all of this, even if we have to detach ourselves from some personal tastes. This means, at a minimum, that we do not allow disputed matters to embitter us. Women's ordination, birth control, sexual abuses, administrative irresponsibility—we acknowledge these critically in all their complexities, but we do not allow them to shape our relationship with the church. Nor do we seize on them—say, on the abortion issue—to cover over other teachings of the pope or our own bishops that challenge us. The death penalty, the admissibility of "preemptive strike" against threatening nations, economic legislation that disfavors the poor and weak—we listen carefully to what the teaching church is declaring in these matters and wish to take any authoritative teaching to heart.

This is not an easy matter. Our faith is enculturated, a good and unavoidable thing, but this requires that mature Christians struggle to be free of the cultural biases woven into our acceptance of the universal values brought to us by Jesus Christ. To add to that, the globalization of culture has diminished many practices and beliefs that once formed a comprehensive Catholic way of life in each nation. To think with the church is to embrace, against local and global cultural biases, what the church has embraced through the ages.

Christians, to begin with, have always asked what they needed from the Father in the name of Jesus Christ. A mistaken scientism, perhaps, has enervated the Catholic prayer of petition. Perhaps science has also lured us away from the corporal expression of spiritual beliefs. We make only a mild gesture at the Lenten fast, which the church cherishes in remembrance of Jesus' forty days in the desert. The church also cherishes the memory of specially chosen disciples, the saints. We do well to keep this crowd of witnesses in our minds and hearts.

Ignatian spirituality holds two human energies in tension: the individual's authentic growth and the community's creative authority. Master Ignatius experienced how God our Creator and Lord deals directly with each person. Yet he submitted even his firmest decisions to the Church's authorities. He could do this because he believed that the same Holy Spirit is creating each individual and also the whole church. The Holy Spirit does not lead us to contradiction and conflict, though we may very well undergo painful tensions as we figure out where the Spirit is leading us. Master Ignatius suffered them himself, being brought before the Inquisition a dozen times.

Thinking with the church is indispensable in an age remarkable for many forms of individualism and also for the insatiable thirst to belong in a community. It enables each Christian to be genuinely individual and yet truly a "living stone" of the church being built, which "offers the spiritual sacrifices which Jesus Christ has made acceptable to God" (1 Peter 2:5).

Finding God in All Things

The hours of prayer during the last days of the Spiritual Exercises are given to the "Contemplatio ad Amorem," the contemplation to learn to love the way God loves. This summarizes the whole experience of the Exercises and furnishes a way to continue living as a contemplative in action. It structures the Ignatian way of finding God in all things.

The contemplation begins with two brief points about what love is. Love is found in what you do, not merely what you claim or declare. And love always proceeds through sharing, each person giving and receiving from the other. With these points in mind, you can reflect on how God loves, and how you can imitate it.

Master Ignatius gives four considerations of the way in which God loves, the first of which goes directly back to the Principle and Foundation. Everything you have and are is God's gift. The whole universe, and everything in it, is a gift given. And God's giving continues, since all things are continually coming to be—and not only things, like rain and music, but also happenings, like a phone call or a visit with a friend. Here is the deepest foundation for the desire that spiritual people feel to give themselves and everything back to God. The yearning is not a kind of self-murder or abasement; it is desiring to love in the way of God, who gives and gives.

The second consideration moves beyond the gifts to their Giver, for God our Creator and Lord remains in the gifts that he gives. Feeling God's presence is easy when we gaze on a crimson sunset above the sea or when we share a gleeful game with someone we love. But we are also given the grace to trust that God is even in untoward incidents. A devout woman conveyed a deep conviction that God was doing something in the tumor in her brain, remaining in it as in all of her. All of us do well to appreciate God dwelling contentedly in the persons closest to us and even in our enemies, even if he does not approve of their acts. A wise old Jesuit priest used to say in the face of puzzling incidents, "I wonder what God is up to?"

He was applying the third consideration about the way God loves. The God whom we hope to find in all things is a busy God. The Lord creates, stays present, governs. God acts directly in each person but also in and through all the gifts we have. We construct a table, and God is making the wood and all the atoms in it. We sing a song, and God is raising the melody. We keep defining ourselves day by day, and God is cocreating us in an asymmetrical but deeply real relationship. Here is the deepest root of the desire to do what God wants and to want what God does. We can hardly force God's hand (a feather resisting a hurricane), but we do help decide how his action will bring earth and its inhabitants to evolve. Loving the way God loves means doing all things well.

A final consideration about God's way of loving: God gives himself. In all that we have and are, we share in God's own gifts. When we are wise, it is with the wisdom of Jesus Christ and his Spirit, the divine wisdom. When we are just, we are sharing God's justice. When we receive Holy Communion, we are sharing in the eternal life of the Son of God. This is not a moral or a political matter; we are created in the image and likeness of the one God, whose entire being is shared among Father and Son and Spirit.

Our being is shared in the same way: we are all more simply human than anything else, born to share the earth and knowledge and love. We are all born to prepare the earth as the banquet table for the kingdom, when all things will be made new. We who are the elect of God are reborn to share the wisdom of God and to be transformed by his flesh and blood, putting off all corruption and putting on incorruption. Then not only will we *share* his glory, but we will also *be* his glory. Praise him. Amen.

Selected Bibliography

Aschenbrenner, George A. *Stretched for Greater Glory: What to Expect from the Spiritual Exercises.* Chicago: Loyola Press, 2004.

Barry, William A. *Finding God in All Things: A Companion to the Spiritual Exercises of St. Ignatius.* Notre Dame, IN: Ave Maria Press, 1991.

Brackley, Dean. *The Call to Discernment in Troubled Times: New Perspectives on the Transformative Wisdom of Ignatius of Loyola.* New York: Crossroad, 2004.

Cusson, Gilles. *Biblical Theology and the Spiritual Exercises.* Translated by Mary A. Roduit and George E. Ganss. St. Louis: Institute of Jesuit Sources, 1988.

Endean, Philip. *Karl Rahner and Ignatian Spirituality.* Oxford: Oxford University Press, 2001.

English, John J. *Choosing Life: The Significance of Personal History in Decision-Making.* New York: Paulist Press, 1978.

———. *Spiritual Freedom: From an Experience of the Ignatian Exercises to the Art of Spiritual Guidance.* 2nd ed. Chicago: Loyola Press, 1995.

Fleming, David L. *Like the Lightning: The Dynamics of the Ignatian Exercises.* St. Louis: Institute of Jesuit Sources, 2004.

Guibert, Joseph de. *The Jesuits: Their Spiritual Doctrine and Practice.* Translated by William J. Young. St. Louis: Institute of Jesuit Sources, 1986.

Ignatius of Loyola. *On Giving the Spiritual Exercises: The Early Jesuit Manuscript Directories and the Official Directory of 1599.* Translated and edited by Martin E. Palmer. St. Louis: Institute of Jesuit Sources, 1996.

—————. *A Pilgrim's Testament: The Memoirs of St. Ignatius of Loyola as Transcribed by Luís Gonçalves da Câmara.* Translated by Parmananda R. Divarkar. St. Louis: Institute of Jesuit Sources, 1995.

—————. *The Spiritual Exercises of St. Ignatius: Based on Studies in the Language of the Autograph.* Translated by Louis J. Puhl. Chicago: Loyola Press, 1968.

Ivens, Michael. *Understanding the Spiritual Exercises: Text and Commentary.* Leominster, England: Gracewing, 1998.

Lowney, Chris. *Heroic Leadership: Best Practices from a 450-year-old Company That Changed the World.* Chicago: Loyola Press, 2003.

Modras, Ronald. *Ignatian Humanism: A Dynamic Spirituality for the Twenty-first Century.* Chicago: Loyola Press, 2004.

Peters, William A. M. *The Spiritual Exercises of St. Ignatius: Exposition and Interpretation.* Jersey City: Program to Adapt the Spiritual Exercises, 1968.

Silf, Margaret. *Inner Compass: An Invitation to Ignatian Spirituality.* Chicago: Loyola Press, 2000.

Smith, Carol Ann, and Eugene Merz. *Moment by Moment: A Retreat in Everyday Life.* Notre Dame, IN: Ave Maria Press, 2000.

Tetlow, Joseph A. *Choosing Christ in the World: Directing the Spiritual Exercises of St. Ignatius according to Annotations 18 and 19.* St. Louis: Institute of Jesuit Sources, 1989.

——. "The Fundamentum: Creation in the Principle and Foundation." *Studies in the Spirituality of Jesuits* 21, no. 4 (September 1989).

——. *Ignatius Loyola: Spiritual Exercises.* New York: Crossroad, 1992.

Toner, Jules J. *A Commentary on Saint Ignatius's Rules for the Discernment of Spirits: A Guide to the Principles and Practice.* St. Louis: Institute of Jesuit Sources, 1982.

An extraordinary spiritual practice
with the power to transform the ordinar

Even in our modern society, one of the most effective ways to
dynamic relationship with God is through the 450-year-old pr
Ignatian spirituality. Joseph A. Tetlow, SJ, a leading expert on the
shows how Ignatian principles and practices can help each of us to discern
God's will for our life and to become a changed person in Christ.

Having overseen the efforts of more than 200 Jesuit retreat houses and
centers for spirituality, Fr. Tetlow is uniquely equipped to describe how the
ordinary person in the 21st century can live out the extraordinary theology
of St. Ignatius of Loyola.

The 40 concise meditations contained in *Making Choices in Christ* explore
what Ignatian spirituality is and isn't; what it means to live by it; Ignatius's
legacy to all who practice the spirituality; and its important concepts and
experiences, most notably the Spiritual Exercises.

An ideal resource to be used before or during a retreat with the Exercises,
this book can guide any layperson at any time toward a life-changing encounter with the living God.

Joseph A. Tetlow, SJ, is currently the director of the Montserrat
Jesuit Retreat House in Lake Dallas, Texas. A former head of the
Jesuit general's Secretariat for Ignatian Spirituality, he has also
served as president of the Jesuit School of Theology at Berk
professor of theology at Saint Louis University, and assoc
editor of *America* magazine. He has written numerous arti
and books, including *Choosing Christ in the World.*

LOYOLA PRESS.
A JESUIT MINISTRY

WWW.LOYOLABOOKS.ORG
CHICAGO

ISBN-13:978-0-8294-
ISBN-10:0-8294-2716

9 78-0-8294-271